Grandad's Girl

EMMA LOUISE

with Asha Mehta

Grandad's Girl

EBURY
PRESS

1 3 5 7 9 10 8 6 4 2

Ebury Press, an imprint of Ebury Publishing
20 Vauxhall Bridge Road
London SW1V 2SA

Ebury Press is part of the Penguin Random House group of companies
whose addresses can be found at global.penguinrandomhouse.com

Penguin
Random House
UK

First published by Ebury Press in 2018

www.penguin.co.uk

A CIP catalogue record for this book is available
from the British Library

ISBN 9781785037641

Typeset in 11/16 pt ITC Galliard Std
by Integra Software Services Pvt. Ltd, Pondicherry

Printed and bound in Great Britain by Clays Ltd, Elcograf S.p.A.

Penguin Random House is committed to a
sustainable future for our business, our readers
and our planet. This book is made from Forest
Stewardship Council® certified paper.

This book is dedicated to survivors who have already come forward. To those who haven't – there is a way to get past it and you will be believed.

This book is a work of non-fiction based on the life, experiences and recollections of the author. The names of people, places, dates, sequences or the details of events may have been changed to protect the privacy of others.

Prologue

I stared hard at the pistachio and cream-striped bed-covers. They were so familiar to me and yet it was as if I was noticing them properly for the first time. They made me recall deckchairs by the seaside, fluttering in a warm breeze. Or sticks of candy cane, the sugar rush making me giddy.

I forced myself to ignore the room I was in, the bed I was pinned onto, the hammering of my heart. I desperately willed myself to block out what was happening to me in that moment, in that bedroom, twisting my neck and turning it away to focus my attention on more of the stripes. Shutting down my emotions and pretending I was somewhere else was how I would cope in the years ahead, to help me survive the sickening world I found myself trapped in – a world no child should ever witness. A world I was dragged into by the one person who should have protected me …

But this time, my powers of imagination failed me. They weren't enough to block out the horrors. It was the minty mouthwash that hit my nostrils and sent me hurtling back into my body and into the vile present. It was on Grandad's breath and I could smell it as he lay on top of me, squeezing my small child's frame.

I froze as he pulled down my pink pyjama bottoms and roughly pushed my legs apart. Shockwaves of searing pain ripped through me. My tears fell silently onto the bed sheets. My innocence had been stolen forever.

At the age of just 11, my grandad Karl, my hero, had raped me.

I was the baby of my family, and my grandad had latched on to my need to be grown up, to matter. He'd lavished me with attention and praise and bestowed on me the pet name 'Grandad's girl'. It was a name that used to fill me with pride, but soon came to mean everything I loathed.

The only way I was important to Grandad was as his sexual slave. When I was 11, he began a process of grooming me that was so masterful and manipulative, no one – not my parents, school, friends or the authorities – guessed what was going on. It must have made him feel utterly untouchable, because soon, raping me was not enough to satisfy his vile appetite.

For too many years, I was silenced. By Grandad and his frightening threats and by my own, all-consuming shame. But I won't be stifled anymore. I am stepping out of the shadows and sharing my story.

The process of writing this book has been painful and torturous, but it is something I was compelled to do. I want to show my grandad that he didn't break me, however hard he tried. I want to highlight the failures of the authorities and society that let me slip through the net. I want to thank my parents for their unending love and support. And I want to do it for me, to help me understand the magnitude of my ordeal and accept that I wasn't to blame.

But most of all, if reading my account saves another girl from a similar fate, I will have fulfilled my purpose.

Chapter 1
Baby of the family

I was never meant to be born. I hurtled into the world defiantly clutching my mum's coil in my tiny, scrunched up hand. When Mum realised her contraceptive had failed and she was pregnant again it took a while to adjust to the shock. But from the moment I was placed first in Mum's arms and then Dad's, a scrap of a thing, I was very much wanted.

I was born on a wintry February day at Lincoln County Hospital. Mum and Dad were childhood sweethearts; they'd been inseparable since the age of 15. The affection they still felt for each other many years on was clear to see, and it spilt over into their fierce love for and protectiveness of their children. They would have moved mountains for us and we felt comforted in the depth of their devotion. Theirs was the kind of idyllic, enduring marriage I dreamt of emulating.

My dad Michael is from Mayo in Ireland and was brought up Catholic. Although he wasn't overly religious, he, Mum, me and my four older siblings always went to church on Sundays. Dad was strict and old-fashioned, believing in traditional values such as that the first person you slept with was the one you should marry.

Dad is one of 16 children and I once overheard him joke: 'There was no TV in those days.' That was the beginning and end of my sex education. No one ever sat me down to have a talk about the birds and the bees. It was just out of bounds, forbidden. Mum and Dad were prudes about that kind of thing.

Mum, Sheena, was a soft touch and I'd go to her when I'd fallen out with someone and needed a hug. 'Don't look back; don't let things worry you, love,' was one of her favourite sayings. I felt supported and safe.

If I was grounded, Mum would feel sorry for me and sneak some sweets into my room. She gave me a backie on her bike and we'd fly through the streets towards school or the park, my arms wrapped tightly around her waist, carefree and happy. I loved how compassionate she was. When I fell over and hurt my knee, she would kiss it better and pretend the floor was naughty for tripping me up.

We were a close-knit brood who lived in a four-bedroom house on an estate in historic Lincoln, but my three sisters – Lizzie, Belinda and Clare – and brother Joe were much older than me. When I was born, Lizzie was four years old, Belinda six, Joe eight and Clare ten. Throughout my childhood, they seemed so much more sophisticated than me and a little out of reach.

As the baby of the family, I was often indulged and doted on. After having my four siblings, Mum and Dad had decided that their chaotic, cherished family was finally complete. But I, feisty and contrary, had had other ideas. As I grew up, I knew instinctively I had to make my voice heard in an already established household. I was often the recipient of my big sisters' hand-me-down clothes or toys, which made me feel I had to fight harder for my parents' love and attention. Maybe the fact I'd been a happy accident gave me a bit of an outsider complex.

One of my earliest memories is of my nan, Grace – Dad's mum – lifting me onto the kitchen sideboard and handing me a present wrapped in a big red bow. Tucked inside was a pretty cotton dress embroidered with roses. I remember feeling ecstatic. This was one of the first things that was mine from the start – not owned by any of my siblings before – and it made me feel special. Grace died of ovarian cancer when I was two, so this was a very early memory.

I quickly learnt I could get more attention from Mum and Dad than my brother and sisters but it came at a price – being resented by my siblings. But they didn't realise it also meant Mum and Dad kept a closer watch on my movements. I could wrap Dad around my little finger, and if I told him about the detentions or other wrong-doings of my elder siblings, such as arguing or smoking, I'd be rewarded with treats from the chippie, corner shop or some extra few minutes playing on the climbing frames in the park. My brother and sisters used to get mad and call me a 'grass', often leaving me in tears. But my parents would tell them off for being naughty and upsetting me and I'd get thanked. In my mind I thought it was best to be honest if I overheard something, so I blurted things out to Mum and Dad. Secretly, it made me feel valued and as if I had a role in my big family. I was often jealous of my brother and sisters' freedom and snitching on them gave me a little taste of it.

My family and I, including my siblings, aunts, uncles, nan, step-grandad and various cousins, spent summer holidays together, travelling en masse to Cornwall, Skegness and the Med.

Holidays were a great time to let loose with my brother and sisters. Clare, being the oldest, was the responsible one. She was a good listener, full of pearls of wisdom that made me look up to her and be a little in awe. My brother Joe was the joker and always had me in stitches with his quick wit. But his humour hid a sharp intelligence; I always knew he could do anything he set out to do. My middle sister Belinda was a ball of fun and laughter and always made time for me. Last, but by no means least, was Lizzie. As the closest in age, she was more like a best friend than a sister. In her dungarees and with her boy mates, she was a bit of a tomboy. We'd have late-night chats in our room, catching up on the day's gossip.

One year, when I was six, 22 of us flew to the Greek island of Kos. It was such a happy time, eating like kings at an all-inclusive hotel with never-ending buffets.

'Dad, I want to jump off the diving board,' I pleaded one day, eyeing up the platform towering above me.

'Come on love, I'm going to teach you how,' Dad said, playfully lifting me up and plunging me into the deep end of the pool. I shrieked with delight and was soon leaping down into the pool like an expert. I was fearless; a natural water baby.

On another holiday, this time in Skegness, Dad pulled a dinghy loaded with the whole family into the water and then tipped it over, sending us flying. But although Dad could be a bit of a joker, friendship came second. He was a father first and foremost.

Only Grandad didn't come with us on that holiday. He and my gran Ellie had divorced before I was born and now she was with someone else. He'd stayed away to avoid encountering any awkwardness when he saw them, but I didn't really understand that then.

On my first day of primary school I was excited but terrified. My mum took me, but when she let go of my hand and ushered me towards the school gates, I burst into tears because she had to leave me. I caught her wiping her eyes before turning away.

It was scary at first but I was soon engrossed in playing with all the new toys. I liked the breakfast club, where I'd make pancakes slathered with Nutella. But I still had pangs of missing Mum.

To get to school, Mum would put me on the saddle of her bike while she pedalled standing upright. One morning, she lost control and we tumbled off. I cut my knees and Mum grazed her face. I remember she was so upset that we had fallen. She cleaned me up, gave me a kiss and bought me a Panda Pop and sweets, which were a rare treat at home. She said I was only allowed them after tea and no more than a couple of sweets because they would rot my teeth. Mum wasn't worried about herself, just me, but I was fretting about her because she was bleeding.

I still had a dummy which my parents tried to take off me. But I would hide it by sneaking it in my school jumper. When I needed comforting, I popped it in my mouth and felt calmer. If I didn't have it, I sucked my thumb.

As time went on, I started feeling stifled by my cosy, sheltered childhood. My parents asked me to leave the room if two characters so much as kissed on TV on soaps like *EastEnders*. I just didn't understand why and would wrack my brain wondering what the point of kissing was and why it was so bad. I didn't know about sex or what it meant. No one explained anything and I felt as if there were so many things that were being kept from me. It was frustrating. Didn't they trust me enough, or feel I could cope with the knowledge?

One day, when I was six years old, I ran up to my sister Lizzie who was playing in the park opposite our home with her friends. 'Want to join our club?' she winked, handing me a cigarette. I found myself nodding vigorously. Desperate to appear grown up and be like my older sisters, I copied her and took a drag, but of course ended up spluttering and coughing. I'd wanted to try it and see what it was like but it tasted horrible. For a moment I'd felt cool and accepted by the group – it was addictive and I craved more of that fleeting sensation. I didn't get a chance to revel in it for long though before my cousin spotted me and ran to tell my parents.

I remember Dad looked furious and disappointed in me, grounding me for seven long weeks. 'I didn't expect that of you, Emma,' he said, his words ringing in my ears. I felt I'd let my parents down. I hated disappointing them. I didn't want them to think that their baby daughter had messed up in some way.

I often resented the fact my older brother and sisters appeared to enjoy more freedom than I did. But deep down, I knew it was because Mum and Dad felt protective of me. As well as being the youngest, I was physically small for my age – although I made up for it in character.

Mum was a cleaner at a school, while Dad developed property. They had five kids and a mortgage so money was often in short supply, but we were always well looked after. I was Daddy's little girl and he'd give me £5 for pocket money, which I'd spend on ice cream and sweets. They'd have handed us their last penny, but we had to do our bit, such as tidying up and other household chores.

I was sassy and had attitude, always wanting to appear older than my years. When I was little, I'd announced: 'When I grow up, I'm going to have boobs, shave my legs and have boyfriends.' I'd seen my sisters shaving and wanted to join in this clandestine and exclusive activity. So one day, when I was seven, I climbed onto the toilet and reached for the razor on the top shelf. Scraping the blade over my hairless leg, the skin snagged and blood gushed out. I yelled out and Mum came running. 'I just want to be an adult,' I sobbed. I longed to be mature and looked up to.

'There'll be plenty of time for that,' she scolded, gently. 'You want to grow up too soon.'

I lived more than three miles from school and, aged 11, I had to take two buses, so I didn't really see many of my friends after school, only the ones on the estate. One game we played was Fox and Hounds. It was like hide and seek but played in the dark, giving it an edge of danger. I would dress all in black and hide in the bush so nobody could see me. The others would count to 20 and try to find me. I was great at finding hidey-holes.

Sally, who had only recently moved onto the estate, was my best friend. I remember one evening, just before dark, we rolled down the hill in the park and looked up at the red sky. 'It's going to be hot tomorrow,' I marvelled at the sunset. Gazing at the gorgeous pinks and oranges in the sky made me feel peaceful and content. Simple things made me happy in those days.

Sally was in a separate class but we hung out together at breaks, playing tig, skipping and What's the Time Mr Wolf? in the playground. We loved pop music like S Club Seven and Steps and spent hours perfecting the dance routines by poring over the videos. We bought *Top of the Pops* magazine and dreamt of being stars. I imagined the adoration from all those screaming fans and being able to travel the world.

One warm day, we pinched a bedsheet from the washing line and made a den in the park. Then we had Ice Pops, snapping them on our knees before ripping them open and slurping the sticks.

We lived in the shadow of the cathedral and its imposingly tall spire in the 'uphill' area of the city. The city of Lincoln is split in two and the uphill section is seen as the more affluent part compared to 'downhill', with its clutch of tea shops, bookshops and independent retailers jostling alongside each other on quaint, cobbled streets.

We sometimes tried to walk up the aptly named Steep Hill, which runs to the foot of the cathedral, gasping for breath when we made it. It really was very pretty but a little wasted on us at that age. We didn't really appreciate it – to us, it was just our boring home town. We didn't see much of it until we were much older, either. On school trips though, I loved to wander the cathedral pretending to be an explorer and trying to find its most famous carving – the cheeky Lincoln Imp!

I wasn't allowed to go into town on my own until I was 12, so the park was the place where most of my childhood adventures unfolded. Saying that, I had to be back in the house on the hour, every hour. If I wasn't, Dad, who had a short fuse, bellowed my name until I turned beetroot and came scurrying back. It could be stifling at times and I often tried to stay out later and later.

Sally's family didn't have very much and so she got targeted by bullies who called her 'fat' and 'dirty'. I felt very protective of her and stood up against them, shouting at them to stop. I hated bullies for making her upset. She was my real friend and I wasn't going to let her get picked on and do nothing. I just thought it was wrong when anyone threw their weight around. I'd always been taught that bullying was wrong and it was drummed into me not to turn a blind eye to it.

I liked sports and looked forward to swimming classes, although I detested the caps, which I felt made me look like a boy. I was chatty and spoke to most people at school, but I didn't confide in many people apart from Sally.

Our first school trip was to Eden Camp, a museum in Yorkshire designed to tell the story of the Second World War. I was around nine and remember being fascinated to learn some Morse code and find out about the Blitz, followed by a trip to the gift shop where I stocked up on pens and jumbo pencils.

From when I was little, I wanted to be a children's nurse. It stemmed from visiting my baby nephew in a premature ward when I was eight. Seeing this helpless little thing hooked up to wires, the blood vessels visible under his translucent skin, was heart-breaking, and from that moment I wanted to do something to help children. It hurt me to see anyone in distress and wanted to make it my mission to ease their pain.

On Sundays, we always went to church. I had my Holy Communion aged six, and when I was ten Dad said I had to go to confess my sins to the priest. Of course, at that age my so-called sins amounted to talking in class or pretending to be ill so I could skip school. 'Wear your best clothes,' Dad said. I found it hilarious as I sat in a box and spilt my secrets to the priest and then had to say eight Hail Marys at the altar. It seemed like a strange game.

Another thing that happened like clockwork was that every Thursday I'd see my grandad. He was my mum's father, Karl, and lived on our street, barely two minutes away from our four-bed house. I could even see his one-bed flat from our living room window. He lived alone and we often popped in and out of each other's homes. We shared a close bond that many grandparents and their grandkids do.

Grandad's sweet jar was always topped up and he was so generous, giving me handfuls of candy when I went over. Knowing there was a limitless supply of sweets at his house made me want to find any excuse to go there. If I couldn't get them at home, I knew Grandad would happily hand me as many as I wanted. He would always come round with huge tubs or packets of sweets on birthdays and Christmas. I will always remember my fifth birthday, when he came round waving a multi-pack of my favourite sweets and bounded towards me with a big grin on his face. 'Happy birthday, beautiful,' he sang, stooping down to blow raspberries on my neck. His prickly stubble tickled my skin and his eyes looked huge and comical behind his glasses. He smelt of Imperial Leather soap and spearmint. I broke into giggles and threw my little arms around his neck. 'Haribos for Grandad's girl,' he said, as I ripped the brightly coloured bag open.

'How was your day, what have you been doing?' he always enquired, crouching down to my height when I was very young, really listening to me – not humouring me – and making me feel important. I drew him pictures and he admired them, telling me they were wonderful and he was so proud of me, that I had the makings of an artist. He came to see me once a week and sometimes twice and we would play with my toys.

One morning, I got a five pence coin stuck in my nose. I must have been about seven. I started to panic as I couldn't get it out. Mum had a terrified look in her eyes. 'You've been so stupid,' she said, furious at me. I felt so childish but I was also scared and in tears. She thought I'd have to go to hospital but my grandad saved the day. He came over because he was going to drive me to school and, quick as a flash, he got it out for me. Suddenly, I was laughing and wrapped my arms around him. What a hero, I marvelled.

Out of all my siblings, Grandad seemed to pay me the most attention. To be singled out by him when I was part of such a big family of strong personalities made me puff out my chest with pride. As far as I could tell, my siblings didn't mind that I was obviously his favourite. They had each other and their friends, and I had Sally and Grandad. I think they let me monopolise his time so that I wouldn't feel left out and, in turn, I felt more bonded to him. Whenever he said goodbye, he'd give me a peck on the lips. I thought the special treatment I received from him must be because I was the youngest in the family and because he felt sorry for me not being taken as seriously as the older ones. There were some perks. It's not all bad being the baby, I smiled to myself.

Some days, I confided in Grandad about my dreams of growing up.

'I want to do everything my sisters do – be an adult, laugh like they do and make myself beautiful,' I'd muse, in total awe of them. Grandad would nod, hang on my every word and say he understood.

'You are growing up in my eyes, Grandad's girl, but nobody else wants you to. You're just the little 'un to them. You don't know how special you are. I love you and, believe me, I know you are turning into an adult.'

I felt a ripple of pleasure when I heard those words and played them back to myself when I was lying in bed at night. Yet underneath all the bravado, I was still a child and very innocent.

One day, I'd been fitted for my new school uniform. Aged 11, I was just four feet tall and so I had to have it adjusted. Running over to show Grandad, I did a little twirl. 'You're such a big girl now, you look lovely,' he beamed, admiringly. He couldn't take his eyes off me; there was a sort of electricity in his gaze. I didn't understand it but it made me feel incredible, as if I was on stage and he was my appreciative audience. I was bursting with pride that my beloved grandad thought I was growing up. I yearned to be taken seriously and I felt that Grandad was one of the only people who treated me as the sophisticated adult I wanted to be. It was such a boost to know I was noticed. He didn't talk down to me. My opinions and observations were listened to and respected. It stopped me feeling like the baby, the joker or the accident. To my grandad, I really mattered.

My early childhood was blissful but as the start of secondary school loomed in front of me like a strange and scary new horizon, everything I knew and depended on was about to change.

Chapter 2

'They wouldn't understand'

In 2005, just weeks before I was due to start secondary school, I woke up one morning and Mum and Dad weren't home.

Nan had come over to look after me and my siblings but she avoided meeting my eye and brushed away my questions. All she told me was that they were at the hospital and not to worry. Eventually, a few fraught hours on, my parents came back and sat me down.

'Your grandad's had a heart attack, Emma, but he's ok,' they said. At 11, I didn't fully grasp what a heart attack meant. I just thought he'd been poorly. It was only later, when Lizzie told me he'd almost died on his bed but Dad rushed in and saved him, that I realised it had been much more serious.

It was frightening, but thankfully he pulled through. I was so relieved. I'd always believed Grandad would be around forever. But this health scare had given me a wake-up call. He came to stay with us and slept on the sofa for a few days until he was back on his feet. I couldn't help but worry about him and wanted to make sure he was ok. I was at his beck and call, clinging to him more than usual. It made me happy to be able to care for him, bring him cups of tea and help him put on his socks. He was a little fragile at first, but he was soon well enough to move back to his flat a few days later.

I could tell Mum was still worried about him, though, as I was, and she regularly popped in to visit him and check he hadn't fallen ill again. She seemed to have a permanent furrow across her brow. They'd always been close, chatting and laughing over a cuppa in the evenings. Grandad would always help Mum if she needed anything. And in turn, she would often confide in him if she had any problems with us kids playing up, certain that she could trust her dad to solve them.

'He says he feels lonely – I feel so sorry for him and wish we could do more,' I heard Mum tell Dad. My heart broke for him.

A couple of weeks passed and the moment I'd been dreading arrived – my first day at my new Catholic school. Starting secondary school is daunting enough but, for me, it was even more unsettling because I didn't know anyone who would be in my year. My best pal Sally wouldn't be there, nor would anyone else I'd known at primary school. They were going to school closer to the estate we lived on. I'd begged Mum and Dad not to send me there but they said it was a good school.

Although I thought I wanted to grow up, I was far from ready for all it entailed. My nearest sister in age,

Lizzie, was in year 11, but she had a boyfriend and her own set of friends – she wouldn't have been seen dead hanging out with her kid sister, and I didn't blame her. We caught the bus together in the mornings, but after that I was all alone.

As it was a Catholic school, we were put in houses named after the saints. There were four – Bernadette, Teresa, Hugh and Francis. I was in Hugh form. We had church twice a week and lessons in five subjects a day.

On the first day, a shy, studious girl called Clare sat next to me and she was the first person I spoke to. We became friends, mainly because we didn't really know anyone else. We clung to each other like desperate shipwreck survivors on a life raft who had been cast adrift from all that was familiar. I wasn't into hair, make-up and clothes like the other girls seemed to be. I never dressed to fit in with the crowd. I looked younger than my years and nothing I did made me look older; my small frame and high-pitched, girly voice always gave me away. At 11, I was still quite naïve and sheltered – essentially still a child. But while my place as the youngest gave me a sense of belonging, now it made me feel as if I didn't fit in.

As the weeks went on, I started to get picked on by some of the other girls. There were two in particular – sisters – who had thick, swishy ponytails and tight shirts that showed off their blossoming boobs. I'd look down at my chest, flat as a pancake, and feel inadequate and far from feminine. I was intimidated by their tall, model-girl looks and the coterie of acolytes who hung on their every word.

But I hadn't thought they would target me. It was a shock when it first happened.

'Hand over your lunch money,' snarled one of the girls, called Tanya, cornering me on my lunch break and holding out her hand. Stunned and too frightened to argue, I gave it to her. I was left with a few pennies to buy plums and a carton of milk that day.

I hoped it was a one-off but it carried on. The name-calling began as soon as the bell rang for lunch. 'Hey, slag!' the sisters would jeer, or they'd brand me fat and ugly. It made me feel so lonely and even more isolated. I started looking in the mirror and noticing flabby bits where there were none. I didn't say anything to Mum and Dad because I didn't want to worry them and didn't tell Sally or other friends for fear of appearing weak, but a bubble of anger was blooming inside me.

I volunteered to stay at Grandad's a few nights a week. Mum had been fretting about him, unsure that he was coping alone. It just dawned on me one day that the best solution for everyone would be for me to stay over with him. I could be closer to Grandad, ease his loneliness, help him around the flat and talk to him whenever I wanted. And it would give Mum peace of mind, too.

'I'll be there to keep an eye on him and I can run over and tell you if he takes a turn,' I said to Mum.

'Thank you, darling,' she said gratefully, readily agreeing to the sleepovers. I didn't mind – I loved spending time with him and he relished my company, too. He always made me feel pretty, complimenting me on my clothes or hairstyle. He talked to me like a grown-up, asking my opinion on things we watched on TV. Plus, I was becoming withdrawn and anxious from the bullying and wanted to hide it from my parents. Whenever they asked me how my day was, I said it was fine and then change the subject.

At first, the arrangement worked well. Grandad was always so happy to see me. 'You're Grandad's little girl, you're always welcome here,' he said, tapping the space next to him on his three-piece suite. I sensed he was lonely, too, holed up in his little flat.

Over time, as the bullies continued to torment me at school, Grandad's flat felt like a refuge from that scary world. I could shut the door on it and be his little girl, lavished with attention and praise.

As you walked in through the door, there was a bathroom to the left with a small window. The tiles had little dolphins stuck onto them and there was also a shower curtain with a dolphin pattern on it – he knew I loved them. The three shelves were crammed with razors, aftershave and shaving foam.

His bedroom walls were cream and his bed was covered in either a green-striped duvet or sheets scattered with blue polka dots. The round bedside tables were topped with lamps with shades made from green cloth and white netting, which matched the curtains. The carpets were light blue, while in the corner near the window sat a small TV set on top of a chest of drawers.

The kitchen always looked sparse, with just a kettle, coffee, sugar and tea jars on the worktop by the cooker. The cupboards in the hallway were filled with hoovers and boxes and his airing cupboard was packed with towels and bedding.

The TV stand in the living room was all shiny and varnished. There was an oval coffee table with ashtrays on either side of it and a fruit bowl in the middle. There was a soft, fluffy rug underneath it that I liked to bury my feet into. There was a cabinet with DVDs, CDs, books, a clock, SIM cards and some cash. Next to the three-seater sofa – cream with pale green stripes and covered with throws – there was a tall wooden lamp stand with a black book and a Yellow Pages stashed underneath.

Soon, I started staying over at Grandad's every weeknight, going back home at the weekend. I still saw Mum and Dad every day, as I had my tea at home. I'd pop to Mum and Dad's after school, have a bath, eat dinner and put on my PJs, before dashing to Grandad's. I began to spend most of my spare time at his flat; I was effectively living there. Mum sometimes said she missed me and we'd hug each other, but she also said she was happy I was there to look after Grandad; that she knew how much I cared about him.

Grandad and I spent most evenings watching TV on the sofa – *Silent Witness* and *Wire in the Blood* were our favourites and it made me feel like an adult as we played detective to try and work out who was the killer. But I'd also watch my kids' shows with him too, like *Hannah Montana* and *Power Rangers*.

We shared the same sense of humour and were often in fits of giggles. He wouldn't tell me off, which made me feel I was a responsible adult, not a silly little girl. One of the films he let me stay up late and watch was *Terminator*. We always made the same joke: 'He took his face off and found he was a robot' but it never failed to crack us up.

We also shared the same bed. Grandad told me no one was allowed to know.

'They wouldn't understand,' he whispered conspiratorially, tapping his nose. If Mum or Dad came over and saw us, he said he'd tell them the sofa was too uncomfortable for me so he'd given me his bed.

'Even though I know you're growing up, they don't see that,' he told me.

One day, I was sat next to the radiator while he was on the corner of the sofa. Looking over at the windowsill, I saw three mobile phones lying on it. As Grandad followed my gaze, he said quickly: 'They're spares in case mine breaks.' I didn't think much of it.

Curious and bored one time, I took the black book from under the lamp stand. 'What are all these?' I said, seeing a scrawled list of names and numbers.

'Don't go looking in there, it's my private address book,' Grandad snapped. I remember vaguely thinking he'd seemed a little touchy about it but soon forgot about it.

Most of the time we got on like a house of fire. I'd tell him what I'd learnt at school, gossip about the popstars I liked and we'd laugh at TV shows. I started having tea at Grandad's instead of at Mum and Dad's some nights of the week. I don't really know why – it just seemed easier and while home was crowded and I had to jostle for attention, Grandad had more time for me at his place. When he cooked, I helped set the table and choose which cutlery we'd use.

One night, a couple of weeks since I'd started staying over, we were on the sofa as usual when he reached into his cigarette packet and pulled one out. 'Here, this is for you,' he grinned. 'I want to thank you for staying and keeping me company.' As I put the fag to my lips and he lit it for me, I felt cool, grown-up and special. Not the meek, taunted schoolgirl or the baby of the family. Grandad seemed to know this and tapped into my need. Compared to when I'd taken my first drag aged six, this was a completely different experience. I felt empowered and so grateful to Grandad for thinking I could handle it. My parents mollycoddled me, but at Grandad's I felt free to do anything and be anyone. It was as if I was living a double life – a child in the day and a young woman at night. It felt intoxicating.

'You're the best, Grandad!' I squealed.

Later that evening, he gave me a glass of a clear liquid in a tumbler. 'Drink up,' he encouraged. I took a sip and grimaced.

'Urgh, it tastes funny,' I said, my throat burning.

'It's vodka and lemonade,' Grandad said. 'You want to be treated like a grown-up, don't you Emma?' he asked, sidling up closer.

I nodded, necking the alcohol. Being an adult like all my siblings and the more worldly girls at school was what I was striving for and when Grandad mentioned it, it stirred something inside me. If this was what I had to do to prove myself worthy of that title, I would do it. Quickly, my head started spinning and I began to feel disorientated. I'd never tasted a drop of alcohol before and didn't understand what was happening, that I was getting drunk.

Suddenly, I felt Grandad stroke my legs. I thought it was weird but told myself it was just Grandad – he had always been touchy-feely.

A couple of nights later, I popped over to Grandad's again. It was Sunday and he usually went out boozing at the social club during the day.

'I'm going to order us a Chinese,' he slurred, grinning.

When the takeaway boxes arrived, he put them on the side, grabbed my head and started wiggling his tongue at me, saying what sounded like 'Hell-ell-ello', coming closer and closer.

Suddenly, he stuck his tongue violently into my mouth and tried to kiss me. I felt strange. My stomach turned in disgust. Then, just as suddenly, he let me go.

I was so shocked and confused, I couldn't say a word.

The taste of his saliva, his bumpy tongue and stale beer made me retch. I was still only 11 and I didn't know what had just happened. He'd always kissed me on the lips, but this was much more intimate. Maybe it was just a progression in our relationship, now that we were getting closer? He'd never put his tongue in my mouth before and I wondered what it meant. I'd never even kissed a boy.

Because it was a Sunday night and I stayed with my parents at the weekends, I went home in a daze, figuring it must have been a drunken one-off. After he kissed me, he was just acting like his usual goofy self, smiling and joking. He'd brushed it off, as if it had never even happened. But I couldn't forget it.

Little did I realise that an important boundary had just been crossed and there would be no going back.

The next day I went to school, where I had to endure more name-calling, and that night I stayed at Grandad's again.

Nothing strange happened and Grandad seemed back to normal. I felt reassured and convinced that the sloppy kiss was a booze-fuelled blip. The following night, Grandad handed me some more vodka as we sat watching TV. I felt a thrill run through me. Even though it scared me, my longing to be taken seriously made me take a sip. I wondered if I'd feel the same strange sensation again. Maybe the second time would be better, like the cigarettes. I tried not to think about what had happened last time we had drunk together. I wanted to stay in the moment and take it in. I wondered how the bullies at school would feel knowing I was drinking alcohol. I felt a part of a secret club. Now I could get a glimpse into the lives of my grown-up sisters.

'I feel funny,' I said.

'It's just the drink,' he replied, smiling.

Encouraged by Grandad's response, I drank some more, starting to enjoy the fuzzy feeling in my head.

I felt braver and less inhibited, and I laughed harder at every one of Grandad's lame jokes. I tried to ignore the sense of foreboding I felt in case it ruined our drinking session.

When the TV programme was over, we headed to bed.

He had on his white t-shirt and blue checked pyjama bottoms, while I had my pink PJs on.

'Goodnight, Grandad's girl,' he said, giving me a peck on the lips as he put me to bed.

Suddenly, he started breathing heavily as his cold, wrinkled hands travelled over my pyjamas.

Lying on my back I turned rigid with fear.

'What are you doing?' I managed to blurt out. I felt sick, confused and frozen.

'It's alright. This is what should be happening with your grandad, Emma,' he said, continuing to feel me up. 'This is normal – trust me.'

I didn't know what to think.

Here was my grandad – my role model – telling me what he was doing was right, when to me it felt all wrong.

I was so confused – maybe this was happening because we were being even closer? Was it just the next step in our relationship?

He got up, opened a drawer and rummaged around before he pulled out a DVD and put it on, continuing to grope me.

I tensed up. The figures writhing around on screen were doing things I'd never seen before. There was a man and woman and they were completely naked. They didn't even have any underwear on and I could see their private parts. I'd never seen a man's bits before. The woman was touching then sucking the man's willy like a lollipop and then he was moving up and down on top of her, making her scream out. At one point, it looked as if he was inserting items into her bits. I wanted to throw up, I was so terrified, but I couldn't tear my eyes away from the screen. It looked as if the woman was in pain. Or was she enjoying it? I was so confused. What on earth was going on and why was Grandad making we watch? And why was he touching me all over?

It felt as if it went on forever.

I fixed my gaze on the ceiling, then the mint-striped lampshades on the bedside tables. Anything to try and ignore what was happening to me. I didn't want to be here. I felt overwhelmed with fear and loathed every single second that I was in the present. To try and stay calm and get through it, I had to focus on something else. This would become my way of coping. My survival mechanism. Focusing on the mundane so that the horror wouldn't touch me too deeply.

He kissed me and then his hand snaked down my pyjama bottoms and into my private parts. Climbing on top of me, he grunted as he forced his fingers roughly inside me.

I flinched from the searing pain which shot through me. I didn't know what to do or how to react. But in the end, I did nothing – lying there helplessly as he interfered with my body.

'Do what she did on the porn film,' he ordered.

Porn. So that's what that horrible DVD was.

As he instructed me to put my hand around his willy and move it up and down, I tried to imagine I was somewhere else – at the beach with my sister Lizzie, playing tig with Sally.

A few minutes later, Grandad sighed heavily. His willy went floppy and some strange, sticky liquid covered my hand. I was so shocked and wiped it on the covers, wanting to get it off me. Had I hurt him? But Grandad seemed content.

Eventually, he turned around and went to sleep, and I struggled to comprehend what had just happened to me. I couldn't switch off. I was in a state of distress, but the tears wouldn't come. I felt too frozen in shock. An internal battle with my thoughts was raging inside me. Surely, what Grandad said must be true – that this is what all granddaughters did with their grandads? I loved and trusted him and he adored me. But I couldn't reconcile this with what he'd done. Why would he lie to me? I kept telling myself it must be normal for a grandad to act in this way, desperately trying to drown out my instincts, which were screaming that this felt very wrong. *Is this what sex is?* I shuddered. I'd always been taught that it only happened when people are married. But maybe this wasn't true after all. I longed to ask my friends if they too did the same thing and just didn't talk about it. But I knew I'd be too scared to ask. Would they think I was disgusting? A freak? My head was spinning. Exhausted from my mental sparring, I fell into a fitful sleep.

The next morning, Grandad acted all chirpy and normal at first – as if nothing had happened. But then suddenly, his tone switched and turned serious. 'I'm making your favourite for tea tonight,' he said. 'See you after school.'

I knew from the way he'd spoken that I couldn't disobey him; I had to be there.

Suddenly, he stared at me intently. 'You know I love you very much, don't you Emma?' he said. 'I know how grown up you are but no one else sees you like that, only me.'

I couldn't shake the previous night's events from my mind. They followed me around like a dark cloud. I felt gloomy and miserable. Then at school, the bullying came to a sickening head.

During Spanish class, I was passed a folded-up note. Opening it, my throat went dry. '*Get raped and murdered*,' said the twisted message.

Raped. What was that? I'd never heard it before but a sixth sense told me it wasn't something pleasant. I screwed up the note and buried it in my blazer pocket, and tried to stuff the pent-up anger and upset down inside me. But I couldn't squash it down any more and in a moment of madness, I slapped one of the sniggering girls. The teacher had her back turned, but the girl glared at me and whispered, 'I'm going to tell on you, just you wait.'

When I went home, I gave Mum the blazer to wash out an ink stain, accidentally leaving the note still inside it. A few minutes later, just as I had left for Grandad's, I got a call to meet my sisters Lizzie and Belinda. I was apprehensive about why they wanted to see me, but I was also glad as I wanted to delay going back to Grandad's after the previous night. I was so mixed up because he'd told me it was normal, but it just didn't feel right to me.

'Dad's found the note in your jacket,' Lizzie said. 'He wants to see you at home.'

'I can't go, he'll be angry,' I panicked.

'Don't worry Emma, he just wants to find out how you are,' Belinda assured me.

We reached the house, and nervously I inched into the living room, where Mum and Dad were sitting on the sofa with sad eyes.

'I can't believe you're being bullied and haven't told us,' Dad said, his voice strained. 'You've got to stand up to them.'

They'd discovered my humiliating secret. I hung my head in shame. He said that they were going to contact the school. Everything in my life was beginning to feel out of control. I felt that I was losing my grip.

Even after what Grandad had done, I didn't stop going back to his. I went because he told me I had to – that he was the only one who saw the real me.

That night for dinner, we had chicken legs with chips and gravy. He used rock salt and it got stuck in between my teeth. To this day, I can't stomach it.

'Have you ever had sex?' he asked, eyeing me hungrily and pushing a glass of vodka towards me.

'No, I don't know what it is,' I said, blushing.

'Oh, I'm sure you have, a grown-up girl like you,' he pressed.

As we got into bed, my heart thudded in my chest. Even in the dark, I could feel the weight of Grandad's stare. His breathing was getting heavier as he inched closer and closer. Instinctively I moved away from him, but as I clung to the edge of the bed I knew there was nowhere else for me to go.

By now, he was almost on top of me. Without uttering a word, he touched me under my clothes and then touched and licked me between my legs.

'Relax, stay calm,' he ordered.

I felt sick and wanted to run into the bathroom and throw up. It hurt so much.

Pulling his trousers down, he grabbed my hand and made me touch his willy. Then, he forced me to put it into my mouth, pushing my head up and down on it. The taste made me recoil.

'I'm going to be sick,' I gagged afterwards.

'It's normal, Emma,' he repeated. 'No one will ever understand the love we have for each other. This is a test to see if you can be a grown-up. You can't tell anyone. They don't see you like I do.'

I longed to be a grown-up and be treated like one. So if this was a test, however awful, I knew I had to pass. But why couldn't I tell anyone? That made no sense to me. Surely it had to be wrong if no one could know? Or was it all part of the test? Were other people going through the same thing, other children in my street, at my school? I felt as if I was in some sort of hell.

The next morning, he got up and made me a coffee. I couldn't face any conversation so I quickly threw on my uniform and dashed out of the door for school.

I'd lost my safe haven. Grandad's flat was now a confusing and frightening place. School was like entering the dragon's den with the bullies, and at home I'd be met with Mum and Dad's questioning, concerned faces. Dad had gone in to talk to the school but it had come to nothing. They'd taken the bullies' side because I'd hit one of them after I got that note in Spanish class about being raped.

This was the first time I'd lied to my parents. By hiding what was going on at Grandad's and the frequency and extent of the bullying I thought I was stopping them from worrying – but it felt all wrong. Once I was at school, the maelstrom of emotions running riot inside me spilt out.

After school one day, I saw one of the smirking sisters – the ringleader, Tanya. 'Hey slag,' she jeered.

That was all it took. Full of rage, I lunged at her, smacking her in the face. A crowd saw us fighting and I was reported to the headteacher. I was suspended for two days.

'I'm glad you stood up for yourself but there are better ways to do it, love,' Dad said.

When I went back, I saw the other sister and lost it. She had been taunting me all day, calling me a bitch and slut, and I couldn't take much more so I waited until we were a little way from school, ran up behind her and thumped her. All hell broke loose when some of the other children saw, and again I was dragged to the head's office.

'If you're trying to get yourself expelled, you're going the right way about it,' she said. No one wanted to hear my story. No one questioned why a normally well-behaved girl had turned violent.

Mum and Dad seemed at a loss. They put my disruptive behaviour down to the bullying. No one knew the real reason because I kept it hidden, but it was there if someone was willing to really look.

Chapter 3

Innocence Lost

A couple of nights later, a Thursday, Grandad stole the final shred of my innocence.

I'd had another miserable day at school trying to block out the bullies' ever-more caustic barbs. But they marked me like bullet wounds. After the fallout from the fights, it seemed as if everyone was whispering and sniggering when I walked past. I'd stopped caring about my hair and it was unwashed and straggly. I must have looked like a tramp.

The week's horrors were weighing heavily on my mind. I'd already brushed my teeth furiously until my gums were sore, desperately trying to wash away the sickening taste of my grandad's privates from my mouth.

At school, I passed a note to the PE teacher. I'd forged my mum's signature and said I couldn't take part in the double session because my asthma was playing up. But actually it was because I couldn't face undressing in front of the other children. I was convinced my body was tainted after Grandad had got his grubby hands on it and that everyone would be able to tell what he had done to me. Instead, I shut myself in the toilets and with the chewable toothbrush in its Kinder Egg-type plastic ball that I'd got from the vending machine, I spent my time scraping my teeth and tongue with the spearmint-flavoured brush. It had become a compulsion but I was determined to keep brushing until I couldn't taste Grandad anymore.

I couldn't eat that whole day either, because my stomach was churning so much. I wondered if I should tell anyone about what had happened, but I was so worried about the repercussions. Even if they believed me, would my grandad get into trouble somehow? Would I be taken away from my family? It would tear them apart. And that thought was so terrifying, it shut down any part of me that was considering speaking out. No, this was something that I had to deal with on my own.

Later, I put on my happy mask and popped home.

'Can I have some change for the chippie?' I asked Mum, as breezily as I could.

'How was your day, love?' she asked, eyeing me closely.

'Fine!' I replied, as I always did, before shooting out of the door.

I played with Sally in the park, talking about her upcoming twelfth birthday party and flicking through her *Top of the Pops* magazine, before buying some chips on the way home and eating them together in the park. For a few precious minutes I felt normal again.

Yet the things Grandad had done to me made me feel distant from Sally and I didn't know how to bridge the gap. Part of me wanted to tell her everything that had happened at Grandad's but I was fearful of the consequences and his warning. I was a good girl who listened to her elders, especially those she loved and respected. So I talked myself out of it, telling myself it would only open a can of worms and throw up questions I couldn't answer. I wished Grandad and I could go back to where we were before, then I wouldn't have to grapple with all these new feelings and experiences.

As soon as the streetlights went on, I had to pop back home, so I hugged Sally goodbye. After a quick catch up at home, I grabbed my bag. 'Just going to Grandad's,' I said to Mum and Dad.

'Your dad will come over for a cuppa later,' Mum said, giving me a kiss.

I didn't even consider not going over there. I just felt I had to or there was a risk he would stop loving me. As he was the person I trusted most, I couldn't let that happen. I needed him and wanted him to tell me everything was ok, that I was still his girl.

At Grandad's, I jumped into the bath, pulled on my pink PJs and chilled out on the sofa. I remember my eyelids were heavy with exhaustion, the events of the past few days weighing intensely on my mind. But somehow, I couldn't break away from him. He had me in an invisible, vice-like grip. I loved Grandad but I loathed and feared him too. In the end, I believed he was the only one that understood me, and the abuse was the price I had to pay for his love and protection.

When Dad came over I aimlessly flicked through the channels while Grandad chatted to him about what was on the news.

'She's not been giving you any grief, has she?' Dad asked him, winking at me. 'She's not been staying out late?'

'No, no, she won't be going out again, she's not allowed,' Grandad said. He wanted to fool my dad into thinking he was looking after me properly. And he was very convincing. To Dad he was all smiles and charm, but when addressing me he turned stern and serious and put on this air of authority so Dad would think he was trustworthy.

Inside, I was willing Dad to pick up on some sign, anything, that would mean he'd take me back home and never let me go back to Grandad's again. But he turned to leave, kissing me goodbye and leaving me to Grandad's mercy.

Climbing into bed, I scrunched my eyelids tight shut and prayed to the God I was rapidly doubting to spare me from Grandad's clutches. If he did save me this night, I'd be good, the best. I'd tidy up after myself, study hard at school and never talk back to Mum and Dad. Only, he didn't listen to my pleas.

'Have you ever shagged anyone?' Grandad leered.

'What does that mean?' I asked, my heart pounding in my chest.

'It's when a man puts his dick into your bits,' he said.

I'd never heard the word 'dick' and thought it sounded weird and the crudeness of it made me flinch. He'd never used words like this with me before. Did he think I was grown-up enough to hear them? If this was what being a grown-up was, it wasn't how I had imagined.

'Are you sure you haven't, Emma?' he pushed. 'You can tell me, I won't say a word.'

The sense of fear and discomfort was overwhelming me.

'No,' I mumbled.

Just as I'd been fearing, Grandad popped a blue, diamond-shaped pill, which he said was called Viagra, and, just as I'd been fearing, switched on his disgusting porn DVD. I'd seen him take the pill before but just thought it was his heart medicine.

I turned away, pretending to go to sleep but my mind was racing. Grandad wasn't going to let anything stop him. He pawed at my nightclothes, removing them completely this time. I froze as he undressed me; I felt totally vulnerable and exposed. Every inch of my skin crawled with dread, anticipating the horror that would inevitably arrive. Ignoring my distress, he used all his weight to pin me to the bed. I shuddered as I felt his withered skin and coarse, grey hair rub against my body. I remembered the smell of minty mouthwash on his breath. To this day, I can't stand it.

When he forced himself inside me, a searing pain that I'd never felt the like of before tore through my body. I thought I would break in two.

'No, it hurts!' I cried, but he carried on.

Paralysed with terror, I was powerless to fight him off. Physically I was tiny but mentally, too, I felt beaten down and drained and had no energy to even figure out how to resist. I stared at the bare ceiling, the striped lampshade, trying everything in my power to avoid his gaze. It felt as if it went on forever.

'Trust me, this is what should be happening,' he grunted.

I was skinny with a flat chest and looked even younger than my years. But Grandad didn't take any of that into consideration. I was too naïve to realise he'd been grooming me for months, possibly even years, plying me first with Haribo sweets, then with cigarettes and alcohol.

After this 60-year-old man had finished having sex with his own granddaughter, I ran into the bathroom and was sick in the basin. My private parts were sore, covered in blood and burnt when I urinated.

'It's normal, this is what happens when it's your first time,' Grandad said when I cried out. He appeared cold and unfeeling. But even then, I still believed he must love me. That's why he was doing this.

Then, I got into the shower and turned it onto the hottest setting I could bear, targeting the showerhead between my legs. Grandad had come inside me and I felt tainted; dirty. I throbbed down below and wanted to soothe the pain.

When I got back into bed, Grandad whispered: 'I am glad I took that Viagra, I was rock solid and you were so tight.'

I didn't really understand what he meant but it made me feel disgusting and uncomfortable. I was light-headed and in so much pain.

'This is what it is,' he went on. 'You're a grown-up, I love you and would never hurt you. You've got to trust me. Good night, my beautiful little girl.'

I felt so messed up. Was this actually wrong? Because Grandad seemed to be suggesting it was normal. Was it my fault? Had I encouraged him?

My head swirled with confusion and anxiety. Why had I just lain there? Why hadn't I put up more of a struggle? I blamed myself. Grandad kept saying I was a grown-up. Maybe I was too grown-up, and that's why this was happening. I swallowed the sleeping pill he gave me and let myself slide into unthinking oblivion.

The next morning, I woke up and, for a few blissful seconds, I was just young schoolgirl Emma with the only thing to worry about being homework and annoying siblings.

Then, feeling something wet and sticky in my knickers, I took a peek and stifled a scream. They were soaked with my blood. It was a horrific reminder that last night had actually happened and wasn't some twisted nightmare. Within a couple of weeks, Grandad had gone from touching me to forcing himself onto me. His corruption of me was so fast, it made my head spin.

I felt drowsy from the effects of the sleeping pill and could barely function. Somehow – I'll never know how I managed it – I put on my uniform and dragged myself to school. Looking back, it was a heroic effort, but at that moment, I didn't know what else to do. Besides, it was a few hours of respite from Grandad, even though I was stepping from one hell into another.

The day passed in a daze. I can't even remember which lessons I had or my bus journey home. As it was a Friday, I went back to Mum and Dad's. I heard their voices in the living room, talking in hushed tones.

'It's just those difficult tween years, and she's been snapping and getting into fights,' Mum said.

That's what they'd put the change in my behaviour down to. I could hardly blame them. I wasn't opening up. I'd shut everything away into a box in my mind. It was the only way I could cope. Mum was right – I'd been talking back to the teachers and giving short, sharp answers when my parents asked how school had been. I was avoiding being around them because keeping up the facade that everything was just fine was getting harder and harder. The reality was, I wasn't coping.

The following week, Grandad raped me again and again, every night. It was relentless.

I kept going back because the only other alternative was going home and I'd have to try and fake being happy. It was exhausting. Plus, if I didn't go back Grandad would spin some lie to Mum about me getting cheeky with him. He always got his own way, I was starting to see.

I did wonder if he'd done this to anyone else. Maybe he'd been with my sisters first. But when I asked him if he had, he denied it.

'I've only had a relationship like this with you, Emma,' he said.

Bizarrely, it made me feel special. There was something about me that had made Grandad choose me in such a way. It was oddly flattering.

It was inevitable that all these pent-up emotions would need an outlet, and they had spilt over in the form of aggression against my playground tormentors. I thought I'd already been punished for fighting the sisters, but there was a nasty shock in store.

One day, I was hauled in front of the headteacher. 'You're going to be taught at the Magdalene Centre for the next year because of your anger issues,' she said. 'You have to remember to count to ten before you react.'

The centre was the school's pupil referral unit. All I knew about it was that it was a joyless, strict place where naughty children went. It sounded terrible and I didn't want to go. I felt a sense of injustice flare up inside of me. Why was I being treated like this? The bullies were getting away scot free while I was getting all the blame. They'd just tagged me as an angry kid; they didn't know the real reason I'd been acting up, didn't want to know. This was something else that had failed me.

At home, I broke down in front of Mum and Dad as I opened up about the extent of the bullying for the first time.

'I thought it would stop, but it was happening every day,' I sobbed.

'Why didn't you say anything?' Dad asked.

'I didn't want you to worry about me,' I said. 'I just thought I should be able to handle it myself.'

In the days and weeks that followed, Grandad raped me every time I stayed over. He'd put on his porn videos, pop a Viagra tablet and then attack me. It had become like a routine now. I still hated it but because I'd become used to it, been conditioned to expect it, it felt more normal. Even then, it still hurt every time and I would often bleed. But even through the pain and negative emotions, I had to keep telling myself Grandad was an honest man I could trust and he loved me, so if this is what he wanted me to do, I had to let him.

But he started growing bolder and even more depraved. As well as pushing his penis into my vagina, he also began forcing it into my bum. He withdrew it before he climaxed and ejaculated over my back. Not even rape seemed to satisfy him.

'Don't worry, I've had the snip so you won't get pregnant,' he smirked. His words threw me into a state of confusion. So what we were doing – what I'd come to realise was sex – could make me pregnant? Suddenly, I remembered Dad saying that this could only happen after marriage. This must have been the act he was referring to, I knew now without a doubt. I didn't understand but maybe I didn't want to dwell on it too deeply, for fear of what I might realise. I shut my body off each time. I couldn't tell anyone. He warned me he would get into trouble and no one would believe me.

'I'm the only one who treats you like an adult, Emma,' was his constant refrain.

A few days later, I was in the bathroom at home and when I pulled my knickers down, they were soaked in blood. I screamed, panicking. I thought I was dying. I didn't know if it was linked to what Grandad had done or not. When Mum found me, I was in a heap on the floor sobbing.

'Oh love, don't worry, it just means you've started your periods,' Mum said, explaining that I would bleed every month and it meant I had started puberty – that I was on the road to becoming a woman.

When I heard that, I started to calm down. It had been a huge shock but if it was a natural part of growing up, it was nothing to be scared of. Mum fetched me some sanitary towels and showed me what I had to do.

Even though I'd started my periods, it didn't stop Grandad from abusing me. By now, Grandad had groomed me so thoroughly, manipulated me so cleverly and abused me to such an extent that I was willing to do virtually anything he asked. I was totally corrupted and deeply sexualised. I felt more aware of my bodily urges and I needed him and his affection, and if he showed it through the abuse, I came to believe I would have to endure it to hold onto his love.

I found myself downing vodka just to numb myself enough to get through it. I'd drink most nights now, even though it felt weird and I didn't really like it. But it made me feel drowsy and sleepy so I could forget everything for a little while.

A couple of months after the first rape, I was playing on the swings in the park. Suddenly, the bar the swings were attached to came crashing down onto my head. I stumbled home, my head thumping, and Mum and Dad rushed me to hospital. I'd suffered concussion and had to stay there for two days. I felt safe for the first time in a long time. The nurses brought me jelly and ice cream and magazines and put on my favourite TV shows. All I could think of was, *Grandad can't get me here.*

For a few days after the accident, I stayed at Mum and Dad's until I'd regained my strength. But then, inevitably, I found myself back with Grandad. Despite everything, I'd come to depend on him and needed him. And my parents had got used to me being there – they'd have found it strange if I stopped staying over. I hoped maybe he'd spare me after what had happened. No chance.

'Are you better then?' he asked, without a trace of concern. 'Well, you'd better be.'

All he was preoccupied about was that I could participate in the unspeakable acts he had in store for me.

Even when I was tiny, I'd wanted to one day get married and have children. I still clung onto that dream, despite what Grandad had done to me.

Maybe that was what kept me going.

Chapter 4

'I'm going to take you to your first man'

One evening, I was sat hugging my knees on the sofa watching TV at Grandad's when he suddenly walked into the living room. He'd just come from the kitchen where he had been cooking dinner and I could hear the chicken sizzling in the pan.

'I want to see you shag another man,' he blurted out, staring at me.

My head started spinning in fear. I remembered he'd used that word 'shag' before. I'd associated it with sex, with what we had been doing together.

Why would he want me to do that? I gulped. *Wasn't he satisfied with what he was doing to me?* I felt so uncomfortable, so panic-stricken, that I wanted to run out of the room and into the cold night air.

'It would be a massive turn-on for me,' he said, ignoring my visible anguish, every word dripping with sleaze.

I didn't know what to say so I decided it was best to keep quiet and not question him. I did that a lot these days.

That night, he attacked me in bed, as he did every night that week, but he didn't mention the other man again. I hoped against hope it had just been a twisted fantasy of his, not something he'd ever dare put into practice …

Walking back from the chippie with Sally one night after school, it must have been October 2005, my phone beeped with a text from Grandad: *You need to come home, we're going out.*

'What's up?' Sally asked.

'It's Grandad, he's taking me out somewhere,' I said.

'Have a nice time,' she said, waving me goodbye. As she skipped away, I looked at her for a moment and envied her innocence and freedom. Our worlds were miles apart, even though we lived on the same estate. After school, Sally would do her homework and then play in the park. She'd watch TV with her parents, maybe squabble with her brother and then be tucked up in bed by eight. Meanwhile, my night would just be beginning.

Thinking about Grandad's text, I actually allowed myself to feel a little excited, imagining all the possible places we might be going. I can't believe how naïve I was then. An evening stroll on the beach? Playing on the arcades? Maybe the man who had loved me as a grandfather was supposed to feel about his granddaughter was still in there somewhere. I had started to doubt that Grandad loved me as much as he used to. How could he when we rarely played with toys or watched TV together? I wanted that Grandad back – I was desperate to win his approval. I thought it must be my fault if his feelings had changed towards me.

As soon as I stepped through the front door of his flat the atmosphere was strange. I felt unsettled, as if there was an impending sense of doom ahead.

'Get changed and get in the car,' Grandad ordered. 'I'm going to take you to your first man.'

'What?' I gasped.

'It's just what we've been doing: having sex,' he went on calmly, as an icy stab of fear seized my chest.

So it hadn't been some half-baked fantasy after all. It was actually going to happen. My stomach churned with dread.

'You know I told you how I'd love to watch you shag another man,' he leered.

'No, no, I can't,' I protested, hyperventilating.

'It's what adults do, Emma,' he said, turning serious. 'If you want to be an adult, you'll do it. It's what you would do if you loved me.'

It was emotional blackmail, but to my young mind my grandad was asking me to do something to prove how much he meant to me. It was a test of my love. Despite the abuse, I still loved him. He was my grandad Karl, my flesh and blood.

I felt really scared, sick and confused then. In my warped world, I couldn't tell right from wrong anymore. By now, Grandad had totally corrupted me and I couldn't refuse any of his demands. And how could I tell anyone? Grandad had warned me it would rip our close family apart, that I wouldn't be believed, and I was scared of going against him. He had a vice-like hold over me. *What would Mum and Dad feel about me if they knew I'd been having sex ... with my own grandfather?* No, I knew their conservative views on sex and how they always avoided the subject. I knew I had to keep this can of worms tightly shut.

Climbing into Grandad's car, menace hung in the air.

'Here, put these on,' he said, throwing a plastic bag towards me.

Reaching inside, I pulled out a short skirt, stockings and a suspender belt. They were black, see-through and flimsy. They looked as if they'd fall apart if anyone wore them. I didn't really understand why he wanted me to change into them but I took off my jeans and top and did as he asked.

Turning towards me, Grandad licked his lips suggestively. 'You look really good, it reminds me of your school uniform,' he purred.

I felt sick and so awkward. Remembering how I thought I was such a big girl when he'd admired my new school uniform many months ago, it now put a whole new spin on it. I could tell that it excited him somehow. My heart was ricocheting in my chest. When Grandad raped me, it was at his house and, despite how horrific it was, I knew him and it had become familiar. What fresh form of torture was awaiting me now? This man would be a total stranger and I had no idea what he wanted from me. I looked out of the window, fighting a rising tide of nausea.

Suddenly, Grandad slowed the car down, flashed his hazard warning lights and pulled into a layby. It was early evening and already dark outside. I could see a van parked in front of us. He got out and said something to a man but I couldn't see or hear anything. As Grandad turned and headed back to get me, it felt as if everything was happening in slow motion.

'Come with me,' he said, taking my arm and leading me out of the car and into the back of the van.

That's when I saw the man for the first time. He was standing there with his trousers and pants down, his privates exposed. He was old, in his fifties, with grey, curly hair and glasses. I glimpsed at his left hand, his fingers fat like cigars. He was wearing a wedding ring.

'You're beautiful,' he said, creepily.

Oh God.

I started shaking uncontrollably.

'Get on all fours,' Grandad barked. I'd heard him mutter to the man that he was my uncle Bob and he had called me by a false name.

Terrified, I did as he said, crouching down on the filthy van floor. Grandad stripped me and positioned himself in front of me, while the stranger crouched down behind. Tears of agony and shame ran down my face as the man licked me between my legs. Then, I was raped by both my grandad and the other man at the same time. I was forced to suck Grandad's willy while the other man had sex with me from behind.

The pain when the stranger forced himself inside me was the most excruciating I'd ever felt. I was crying so hard, I couldn't stop. But neither of the men – the paedophiles as I'd later find out they were called – cared about my torment. The only way I could get through it was to not feel, so I detached myself from my emotions by thinking about nothing; shutting down my body and mind. It still hurt, but by cutting myself off from my emotions it put a distance between what was going on and how it felt. The experience seemed to last a lifetime, but in reality it was over in five minutes.

'You were amazing, I'll definitely see you again,' the man said to me, zipping up his flies.

I felt totally broken; a shell of the girl I used to be. I didn't know who I was anymore. I felt violated and numb. I knew I would never be a little girl again, finding pleasure in pop music and dancing. Those things seemed like activities I did a lifetime ago when I was pure and innocent. I felt dirty and permanently tainted. My carefree childhood had well and truly been stolen from me.

'Get dressed,' Grandad said, more softly now because, in his eyes, I'd performed well and done my job. 'You're a good girl.'

I was in a state of shock as I stumbled to the car and it felt as if my body was on fire. Grandad drove to Tesco and bought 200 cigarettes.

'These are for you,' he smiled. I realised with a lurch that they were my payment for having sex with him and the other man.

Looking down, I could see blood seeping through my jeans. The man had raped me with such violent savagery he'd split my genitals.

Back at the flat, I went straight to the bathroom and filled up the bath with hot water. I felt grubby and wanted to wash every disgusting trace of my encounter away.

The pain down below was so immense, I had to inch into the water gradually because it stung so much. Within minutes the water had turned bright red with my blood. I stifled a scream. I just wanted the world to stop turning. I was crippled with pain and had so many cuts between my legs. He'd torn my private parts because of how big his willy was.

Sat in the bath, I wanted the nightmare I'd been plunged into to be over. But even then, at such a low ebb, I didn't want to die. I loved my parents so much, I didn't want them to be upset. All it would have taken was for me to reach for a razor and take it to my wrists. But their love – and my determination to live – saved me that time.

I didn't want to be anywhere near Grandad the next morning. Just the sight of him made my skin crawl. I was still suffering from the aftermath of the brutal attack the night before. I couldn't have a wee without it burning. I'd started bleeding again and my private parts were itchy and sore. There was also a white discharge.

'I'm going to have to go to the doctor,' I said to Grandad.

'You're not allowed to say anything about what happened, do you hear me?' he warned. 'If you do, they'll believe me, not you. I'm the adult. You'll be sent away from your parents for a very long time.'

By the time he'd finished his terrifying rant, I was quivering with fright. All I could do was nod. Later, I lied to my mum about it, saying I thought I had a urine infection. *How can I explain the real reason?*

'I'll make an appointment for today,' Mum insisted when she saw me grimacing.

Part of me was exhilarated – surely now, I'd be saved? The doctor would realise I'd been raped and I'd be looked after and never have to see Grandad again.

Later, in the doctor's surgery, I gazed pleadingly at the doctor as he said: 'Are you sexually active?'

'No,' I blushed.

What else could I say? I was 11 and my mum was sitting beside me. I was too embarrassed, too scared, Grandad's threat echoing in my head.

To my shock and disbelief, the doctor didn't examine me. He diagnosed a urine infection, impetigo and thrush, and sent me home with antibiotics. I felt let down again and horribly trapped. *Is this my life now? Why can nobody see what is going on?* But Grandad's manipulation put paid to anyone finding out. He forced me to act normally when I was at home so my parents wouldn't get suspicious.

'If they think there's something wrong, they'll start asking questions and you know where that will lead. No one will understand the love we have for each other, Emma. You'll be sent away and never see your parents again and your dad will kill me.'

I didn't fully understand why but the threat hanging in the air made me feel sick with fear and guilt, so I kept quiet. I had to smile, chat to Mum and Dad about my siblings, about school and not say anything that gave the game away. I had to paint a grin on my face. However much I longed to hide away in my room, I couldn't. I had to face Mum and Dad's questions about my day with a feigned cheeriness that drained me. He would pretend to Mum and Dad that I was grounded and he wouldn't let me have my phone. Grandad knew their movements. That's why they never caught us. It was another reason why I felt so helpless and trapped.

My siblings were so much older they would go into town, but I still wasn't allowed, even in the daytime. When they planned a night out, they'd promise, 'You can come with us when you're older.' Seeing my sisters bowl down the stairs in a cloud of hairspray and glittery make-up made them look impossibly glamorous and exotic. Even at the tender age of 11, I longed to go with them to clubs and restaurants, instead of being left alone with Grandad. Lizzie was spending a lot of time with her boyfriend by then and was barely around, and Joe and Clare worked and had busy social lives.

While I was on antibiotics and healing, Grandad grudgingly stayed away from me. I still stayed over but he didn't touch me and barely engaged in conversation. His attitude changed. There were no more 'Grandad's little girl' comments. Instead, he was ratty and mean.

'I hate not being able to do anything with you,' he said.

I could barely walk – he knew I was no use to him just then. The respite felt blissful, but I knew it wasn't going to last.

At school, I'd swig the vodka Grandad gave me and smoke fags in the toilets or in the fields with a girl called Beth who was in the year above and who also smoked and drank. I tried to hide it and I was good at it – no one picked up I was drunk.

My time in the Magdalene Centre, a cold cabin, was lonely and uncaring. I had to eat my lunch alone, before the other kids had theirs. There were two or three other 'naughty' children in the centre, but we were mostly kept apart. I was upset that I was separated from the other pupils. I lived for the walks to and from school, where I'd catch up with friends and talk about our days.

Somehow, in the thick of this depravity, I managed to enjoy Sally's twelfth birthday. We went to a play centre which had slides, swings, spooky mazes, crawl tubes, a spider's web and air cannons. We might have been two of the older kids there, but we loved it and felt as if we were six again. It was a little bit of normality and I clung on to it tightly. Sally had started smoking now, too – like me, she'd wanted to join the cool, grown-up gang. I liked sharing this with her. It helped strengthen our bond.

A few weeks later, when I had recovered from my infection, I had no excuse not to go on more late-night drives with Grandad. He took me to various sites near the RAF base, a picnic area, woods and laybys to have sex with strangers three to four times a week. They were quiet, secluded locations where people went to 'dog' – meaning having sex with complete strangers or to watch strangers having sex.

The second man he took me to opened the passenger door of Grandad's car and stood there ogling me. He started stroking my leg up and down and kissed my cheek. It felt as if he was checking the goods to see if I made the grade.

'Go into the bushes and do what I showed you,' Grandad forced me.

Terrified, I did as he said. The man grabbed my hand and made me stroke his willy up and down until he climaxed. Grandad just watched this time.

The visits soon became my new routine. When we arrived at the sites, Grandad flashed his hazard warning lights to let punters know we were ready. Sex would take place in cars or the backs of vans and usually involved old men, and Grandad often joined in.

Grandad arranged all the meetings by phone. I had no idea how he knew this vile ring of child abusers, but I now knew what that black book I'd discovered stashed on top of the Yellow Pages was for, though – it was a filthy record of all the men he'd sell his own granddaughter to. I also gathered that he arranged these meetings on his 'dirty' phone, the spare one I'd seen on his windowsill.

I wondered if there were other girls but Grandad said it was only me. Naïvely, I believed him. I couldn't help wondering who these men were. Sometimes, it was with the same men, but other times they were new. I didn't know how he found these vile individuals. Was Grandad the leader of a horrible gang? Did they do it with other girls and how often? If they had daughters themselves, did they not wonder how they would feel? Were they married and did the wives have any inkling?

He started making me keep my school uniform on as a treat for his clients. He led me down dark lanes with a flashlight and then crawled into bushes so we wouldn't be seen. A man I could barely see would be stood with his trousers around his ankles. It always happened outside so there was the added fear of being caught. I'd feel sick and terrified but I'd feel Grandad's hand in the small of my back and the weight of his stare boring into me.

'Go on girl, do it,' he'd order.

By November, he'd pulled me out of lessons to go to the twisted trysts, saying I had hospital appointments. School never questioned it – I wish they had. They had dismissed me as an unruly kid and it felt as if they'd washed their hands of me.

I knew I couldn't break free on my own. By now, I was totally beaten down by the relentless abuse.

Grandad had started telling me Mum and Dad hated me, that they didn't understand me or what I wanted. It really hurt me and I believed it must be true. Maybe my disruptive behaviour had driven a wedge between me and my parents. It made me feel guilty for pushing them away and made me even more reliant on Grandad.

'But I will look after you and give you money,' he said. 'I'm the only person you have.'

He showered me with Nike Air trainers and Playboy tops to buy my silence. I liked having the latest things and so it was an effective tactic.

At the same time, he got really angry if he thought I'd been talking to boys. One day a cousin of mine saw me with Beth at the shops, and a boy was with us. Grandad must have found out through the family grapevine because when I got in, he was furious.

'You're not allowed to talk to boys, it's naughty,' he raged. 'You're a slag if you do that,' he said. He seemed jealous. He was so angry and I got into so much trouble, I believed that what he said must be true.

For half my life, I was Emma the schoolgirl, but for the rest of the time, in this twisted twilight world, I led a secret life as a child prostitute. Grandad was always with me, making me wear suspenders under my school uniform and taking photos. I had to act as if I knew what to do with their bodies, as if I enjoyed it, and to give them what they wanted. Grandad was selling me to these men. I didn't really understand that then, but he was effectively my pimp and he was running a child sex ring involving dozens of paedophiles.

Once, he brought over a piece of paper from the car with a list scrawled onto it. Peering across, I was shell-shocked. It was a 'price list' for me – ranging from £10 for a blow job to £50 for full sex. When I heard him reading it out to a client, I wanted to be sick. I questioned whether he had the list all along but Grandad insisted he hadn't. I think it was because he wanted me to think he hadn't planned all this, that it was just spontaneous. Maybe that sounded less evil. The man said he wanted a blow job. He was so matter-of-fact about it, as if he was ticking off items on a shopping list.

Most of the men had wedding rings on, many were dads and grandads themselves. They must have known I was only a child. *How can they abuse me and then go back to their families as if nothing has happened?* Because by now, I was pretty sure it was wrong. What sort of perverted pleasure are they getting from attacking a child?

After another sordid session, Grandad threatened, 'No one will ever understand. If you tell the family, they'll kill me.'

He laid a massive guilt trip on me so I never felt I could breathe a word. This had become my new normal; it was my way of life now and I saw no way out.

One day, I walked into the kitchen and opened a drawer. Inside, was an empty bottle labelled 'Spanish Fly'. 'What's this?' I asked Grandad.

'It's just for a mate of mine in Benidorm, to help improve his sex life,' he laughed. He said it was like Viagra and boosted performance in bed.

I didn't want to know anything more, so I left it at that.

On one of our visits to a dogging site, I noticed Grandad was jumpy with excitement. With a horrible twist in my stomach, I realised why. There were five men waiting for me. I had to stop myself from throwing up there and then.

I felt as if I was a defenceless animal being encircled by a pack of menacing hyenas. Grandad undressed me and positioned me where he wanted me. I felt so scared and vulnerable and didn't know what to do or why there were so many men there. One was either side of me, Grandad was in front, one was underneath me while another stood over.

Several men raped me as I cried and screamed for them to stop. I wasn't sure if I believed in God anymore, but at that moment, as the men violated my body, I prayed to my dead nan and grandad. I couldn't understand how my own relative could make me go through this torture.

But he was my grandad and I didn't want to get him into trouble. So I stayed tight-lipped and endured night after night of unspeakable abuse.

In February 2006, five months had passed since the start of the abuse and I turned 12. Family came over, handing me cards with money in them. Mum took Sally and I to the cinema where she bought us popcorn and Ice Blast lollies. Grandad had got me Haribo sweets and chocolates like always. Later, he gave me a card addressed 'To my beautiful girl', and handed over dozens of cigarettes.

While other children were playing computer games or going on family holidays, I'd been caught in a murky underworld that I didn't even have the words to describe. The abuse had a profound and damaging effect on me mentally which would haunt me for many more years to come.

Chapter 5
'Good girl'

I'd been shipped off to the closeted Magdalene Centre in a bid to control my 'anger issues', as the teachers called them, but even in this grim solitary confinement where I barely saw, let alone spoke to, a fellow pupil during classes, I couldn't completely shake off the bullies. Wherever I went at break and lunchtime, girls shot me dirty looks or spat venomous barbs in my direction. Maybe I gave off some sort of vibe but they flocked to me like menacing moths to a flame.

The only outlet for the horrendous abuse I was experiencing at Grandad's seedy flat and on our sordid night-time visits was a red mist that would descend whenever the other pupils pushed me over the edge. Sometimes, it would spill over into violence. I can't describe it completely but it's as if I'd see a flash of blinding light and then I'd be out of control, fists flailing. It was like the knot of pain, anger and torment, that had formed inside me since the abuse started and was growing bigger and bigger, would burst out now and again like the creature from the *Alien* films, wreaking havoc and mayhem in its wake.

One such incident involved a new friend, Carly. We both preferred playing outside to discussing boys and make-up. She was timid, tall and friendly. She came up to me one afternoon at school, a look of agitation on her pretty face.

'What's wrong?' I asked, watching her fidgeting fingers with concern.

'A girl in the year above us jumped me yesterday,' she whispered, her eyes darting from side to side as if to check the coast was clear. She looked terrified. 'She said I'd been getting too friendly with her boyfriend, but I'd just been talking to him.'

I felt shocked and upset to see her so troubled and put a comforting arm around her. I'd always had a strong protective and nurturing instinct for those who are weaker than others and couldn't help sticking up for the underdog. It's why I also had an urge to mother younger kids and, despite everything that had happened to me since my innocent childhood days, part of the reason I still dreamt of becoming a paediatric nurse. In a way, perhaps that ambition burnt even brighter now, looming ahead of me, just out of reach, like a tantalising escape route from this nightmare I'd found myself in.

Throughout that day, the sense of injustice on Carly's behalf built up inside my chest and bubbled away furiously. After school, we caught the bus home together. Suddenly, Carly grew tense and her breathing became shallow.

'She's over there, the girl that flew at me yesterday,' she babbled, panicked, gesturing a few seats ahead of us.

Without thinking, I strode over to the older girl. 'Why did you do what you did to my friend last night?' I demanded.

She squared up to me, her face inches away from mine, and something inside me snapped. Grabbing a clump of the girl's hair as she reached for a fistful of mine, we ended up embroiled in a fight. Elbows were flying in all directions and the next thing I knew, she screamed out in horror. 'My nose, it's broken!' she yelled. Blood gushed from her nostrils like scarlet ribbons, making me stop in my tracks and hold back a wave of nausea.

What have I done? What is happening to me? Who have I become? I can't recognise this person, full of rage and hate. Everything is spiralling out of my grasp.

The police were called and I had to go to the station with my dad in the back of a van, head bowed and my face flushed crimson with shame. He could barely look at me and shook his head in disappointment. It hurt to see that I'd let my parents down. All I wanted to do was make them proud of me.

'We will be investigating this,' the officer said, gravely.

Back home, Dad couldn't hide his feelings and they exploded in a fit of temper. 'I'm not impressed with your behaviour at all, Emma,' he raged. 'You should have walked away like I always tell you to. You're grounded.'

'You could get a criminal record,' Mum scolded, looking at me as if she didn't know her own daughter. I felt a pang of hurt. 'What's got into you, Emma? Just tell me,' she pleaded.

Oh, how I longed to pour my sick secret out and have my parents scoop me into their arms and rock me like I was a little girl again, promising that I'd never have to see Grandad again and that everything would be ok.

But before my lips could even form any words, Grandad's stern face flashed into my mind and his repeated warnings ordering me never to breathe a word, that I'd be taken away from my family and would never see them again, rang out. It was enough to shock me into silence. I promised myself and my parents that I would try and avoid trouble, but it just seemed to follow me round lately.

A few days later, it was the anniversary of my beloved nan Grace's death and memories of her had been playing on my mind. I liked seeing her smiling face with kind eyes in photos Dad had at the side of his bed. Mum and Dad had told me amazing stories about her, her caring presence and how much she adored me and always looked out for me. If only she was alive and here now, I wished to myself. Maybe she could have saved me.

I was talking to a friend about her on the bus home from school when another girl from college in the seat behind us started laughing, as if she was mocking my grief.

'Your nan's dead, your nan's dead,' she jeered, nastily.

Pumped up with fury and with hot tears springing to my eyes, I turned and flew at her. It was just tame this time, just some hair-pulling, but they kept taunting that it had all been captured on CCTV so I had no choice but to admit I'd done it. I was mortified.

Back home, seeing the dishevelled state I was in, bruised and damp with tears, Mum and Dad tried to calm me down. They were so worried about what would happen to me if I carried on my volatile behaviour. In the end, to my relief, the police gave me a reprimand. It would stay on my record for five years but I wouldn't be charged.

Meanwhile, Grandad's grip over me was tightening like a vice. His favourite dogging site to take me to comprised two L-shaped laybys near the RAF Waddington base. There were plenty of trees and bushes to provide cover for the murky activities he forced me to be part of.

I remember the car lurching as it hit the potholes on the way to the encounters with the men he'd lined up, making my already nerve-jangled insides even more knotted with dread. There were farmers' fields nearby and RAF police often came down the tracks on patrol. I secretly hoped and prayed they'd catch me with the men in the act, however humiliating that would be, and put an end to my ordeal forever. But Grandad was too clever for that. He was an expert at time-keeping. He made a note of when the officers usually came out to the area and, if they saw us, he pretended we had casually stopped for a bite to eat. Other times, I was desperate for a wee but he would make me wait until the coast was clear, then eventually let me relieve myself in the bushes.

I couldn't blame the police for not being suspicious. All they saw was a kindly and harmless old man and his smiling granddaughter. How would they make the leap to us being part of a seedy child sex ring?

One time, Grandad let me drive his Cathedral City work van down a track and I almost crashed into a metal pole. These rare concessions he gave me were just an illusion of freedom; they were really just clever tactics to keep me under his control.

At some point, Grandad started inviting men over to his flat to pay to have sex with me. I didn't know what he did with all the money. He never told me and he didn't seem to splash out on many things.

He was becoming so brazen. He thought he was untouchable and who could blame him? No one in the entire world knew about his vice den. The rules were that the men weren't allowed to come inside me, they had to wear condoms so there was no risk of pregnancy or sexually transmitted diseases, and they were banned from kissing me on the lips. Only Grandad was permitted to do that. Grandad would watch the punters molest me and, after the men had paid, he'd throw a handful of notes at me – my cut – which I'd usually fritter away on cigarettes and booze to numb the pain.

When a client arrived, Grandad instructed him to park his car elsewhere so Mum and Dad wouldn't wonder who the visitors were. He'd ask the man to leave his car at the top of the road and walk through the gate leading to the flat. Grandad would have parked his car a few streets away and drew the curtains so Mum and Dad would assume we were out.

The first time a man came to the flat in the day time, Grandad seemed nervy, constantly peering through the window to make sure my family weren't around. How true a saying it is that you never know what is going on behind closed doors. My family were just metres away but completely in the dark about my double life.

'Right, I want you to take off your clothes and lie on the bed naked,' he ordered, gruffly. And then softer this time: 'Be a good girl for your Grandad.'

I knew there was no point in refusing. By now, my self-worth had been trampled into the ground and I had no strength to resist. But however much I'd trained myself not to feel, I couldn't stifle the jolt of fear that shot through me as heavy footsteps padded along the hallway.

Seeing me stiffen and curl into a ball, Grandad glared at me fiercely, looking daggers. 'Don't let me down, girl, or there'll be trouble,' he hissed, his jowls wobbling like jelly.

Suddenly, the door creaked open. The man that walked or, more accurately, lumbered in, wasn't as old as most of the men I usually saw. He had jet black hair, a white shirt and black trousers with chains trailing from the pockets, like a prison officer's uniform. But he was fat, rolls visible under his shirt, the buttons straining to contain his bulk.

I wondered, maybe, as he was younger, if he would be kinder in some way. Perhaps he'd take pity on me. But there was no such luck.

'You're so sexy,' he leered as he unfastened his belt.

He pushed his willy into my mouth, while I touched myself – something Grandad had ordered me to do. I didn't feel turned on, though. It was all for show.

I tried to remove myself from the situation, from the four walls. In my head, I was running in the park, my blonde hair flying behind me as I played football in the park and then the Fox and Hounds I played with my friends on the estate. It was my happy place where I felt free and safe. No one could hurt me there.

Minutes later when the man had got what he'd come for, he pulled up his trousers while smirking at me, making my skin crawl. I lay on the bed quietly, not knowing what to do or say. I shrank away from the men. I loathed them from the depths of my soul. Were all men this evil and predatory? It seemed as if they were.

After every mauling, I felt disgust and annoyance at myself, too. Why couldn't I just walk out, fight the men off and go back to Mum and Dad? I couldn't ignore the gulf that had opened up between us, full of everything unspoken. I didn't blame them in the slightest for not working out what was happening and protecting me. I was hiding it so well and Grandad had manipulated them so cleverly by pretending everything was fine, it would have been a miracle if they had found out. I can't explain it properly, but I felt paralysed. And how was I supposed to skip back into Mum and Dad's arms, be their little baby again, when I'd been privy to things no child should ever have to see? Things had gone too far. There was no going back for me. I knew that. The scars from the abuse were etched deep into my psyche.

Grandad, telling the man to call him Uncle Bob, chatted and joked with him as if he was shooting the breeze with a mate down at his local pub, instead of a man he'd pimped out his own granddaughter to. After walking him to the door he came back to the room and grinned.

'Good girl, you did good,' he said, pleased with me.

That night, not content with getting his perverted pleasure from watching me be abused by another man earlier in the day, he raped me himself.

Despite Grandad's meticulous planning and gimlet-eyed watchfulness, becoming familiar with the comings and goings of our street, there were two times when his cover was almost blown.

One afternoon, my uncle popped in unannounced. Earlier, Grandad had pulled me out of classes in the middle of the day after telling the school I had a hospital appointment. He wanted me to be ready for a client, but he was forced take evasive action.

'Hide in the airing cupboard,' he said to me as he hurriedly pushed me inside and shut the door. I was bundled into the pitch black, cramped space, where I had to stay for almost an hour as Grandad spoke to my uncle and acted as if everything was normal. I longed to be found out but I was too frightened to make a sound.

Another time, it was my dad that came over while I was at Grandad's when I should have been in school. I had to jump in the bath and hide behind the shower curtain until Dad had left. It was torture knowing he was there but couldn't do anything to rescue me. I wanted to cry out 'Dad, I'm here, save me from this monster!' but I was frozen by fear.

Many years later, I learnt that my behaviour could be explained by the psychological phenomenon known as Stockholm syndrome. When people are forced into a situation where they have little control over their fate, they are intensely afraid of their captor and have the threat of physical harm hanging over them, they form a sort of alliance with their abuser as a survival strategy.

Grandad was my captor and he had pulled the wool over everyone's eyes so completely and convincingly, no one had a clue what was going on right in front of their noses.

Alongside the relentless depravity, and the sick realisation that I'd been sold for sex for over a year, my life was punctuated by snatches of normal life which kept me from drowning in a pit of despair. One such occasion was my thirteenth birthday party. It was the first time I'd been allowed to go into town with a friend, just the two of us. In the morning, Sally and I excitedly charged around the shops, stocking up on sweets from Poundland. My pocket money had been upped to the princely sum of a tenner a week. Later, Mum stuck magic candles on my birthday cake – I was still deemed young enough for those – and I tried to blow them out as everyone cheered and wished me happy birthday.

There was a family meal and then a trip to the cinema, where Mum bought me a special kid's pack, including sweets, popcorn and a drink. She took me shopping, where I picked out new pyjamas, t-shirts, jeans and shoes. For the first time in a long time, I felt like I was just a normal young girl – just spending quality time with Mum on my birthday. I was special, not dirty, again.

As my body started to develop, I struggled to feel comfortable in my own skin. My boobs were still small and I was very short. Compared to the girls in teen magazines, with their long, lithe limbs and full chests, I felt ugly and insignificant. I was filled with self-loathing. I rarely felt any sexual urges for boys my age because I hated my body. I constantly felt tainted.

Grandad was getting ever more animalistic, biting my boobs and raping me in the daytime, too. Instead of restricting his attacks to the bedroom, he'd put the pouffe on the armchair because I was so small and force himself into me. He'd often make filthy comments about my school uniform.

'I love seeing you in your tight shirt and short skirt – it gives me twitches and makes me so horny,' he said.

Every morning when I walked out of the door, he'd wolf-whistle and waggle his tongue out of his mouth like a lust-crazed maniac. The impact of all this on my self-image was disastrous.

Standing in front of the mirror naked, I examined my vagina, or 'my bits' as I labelled it. It looked so swollen and ugly in my eyes. I'd lost count of how many men had used and abused me and when I glanced between my legs, it was as if they had branded me.

The shame was overwhelming. Scanning my bony frame, I stopped at my breasts. Small and modest, I hated them. My underdeveloped boobs made me feel like a pre-pubescent boy.

There was something Grandad had started to do which I detested almost as much as his violation of me. He'd started to profess his love for me, as if he was my boyfriend. It made me feel horrified and I'd fall silent, trying to block out his sick declarations.

One night, after molesting me, he said: 'I love you so much. One day, you can be all mine. We can go away together somewhere far away where no one knows us.'

The thought of it turned my stomach. He was saying he wanted to make me his wife. There was no way on this earth I would allow that. I still fantasised about falling in love with a boy and starting a family. Whatever Grandad had taken from me so far, including my virginity, my childhood and my dignity, that was one thing he would never be able to steal.

He would have to kill me first.

Chapter 6
Broken

And so the days rolled by, merging into each other.

Every evening after school, Grandad forced himself onto me and then sold me to old men under cover of the starry, Lincolnshire night sky. I was well and truly trapped. He had an insatiable appetite for sex and watching others rape me. He never let up in his search for ever more men – more monsters – to prey on his own granddaughter. The men I was made to have sex with were all different: fat, thin, short, tall, bald and greying. Many were married. Some I saw again on a handful of occasions, others were total strangers.

A few of them were suited and booted, while others wore scruffy overalls with grease stains on them. They'd arrive in a range of different cars – some shiny and gleaming, others beaten up old rust-buckets. I'd find it odd when some of these filthy old men would have pristine nails, immaculate ties or baby-soft hands. It didn't fit with the picture, some-how. It was strange the little details I'd remember, that got lodged in my brain like a stubborn house fly. I think I fixat-ed on seemingly ordinary things as a way to try and detract from the horrific ordeal I was going through.

I noticed that all the men I was sold to were white, though. To add to his many despicable traits, Grandad was a virulent racist. I remember him yelling at me to 'turn that n***** shit down' whenever a song with a black singer came on the radio. I didn't understand why he hated them, but he was from that older, more ignorant generation. Lincoln didn't have many black or Asian families at the time and what Grandad didn't know about, he feared.

Meanwhile, he was becoming ever more depraved.

One day, we pulled up outside a shop off the motorway with blacked-out windows. The sign across the top read 'Simply Pleasure'. Fishing out some tokens he'd cut out of the *Daily Sport* or some other smutty newspaper, he told me he'd be back in a few minutes.

When he got back into the driver's seat, he had a leer on his face. I knew what it meant.

'I want to use these toys on you,' he said.

'What?' I asked, not understanding.

He shoved them towards me as I stared at them, goggle-eyed and scared. One was blue and shaped like a dolphin, another looked like an egg. I was so confused. For a split-second, I thought he'd bought me some toys as a gift. But when Grandad saw my excited face, he roared with laughter. 'They're sex toys, Emma, they're for adults like me and you, not little kids.'

He explained they were called names like vibrators, love eggs and cock rings. I was 13; it made little sense to me.

Suddenly, he grabbed my wrist and glared at me. 'You're to use them on yourself, on your bits, before you see the men,' he said. 'It'll get you turned on and ready for them.'

I didn't really know how to use them but he switched on the vibrator and showed me.

As Grandad drove me to the twisted rendezvous, I used the buzzing sex toy on myself. It felt weird and I shivered. It was unpleasant and uncomfortable and I couldn't understand why it made me clench up. I didn't derive any enjoyment from it at all. I didn't know how much lower he could make me sink.

As we neared the layby, he stopped beside a tree stump.

'Go, they're waiting,' he said, ignoring my tear-stained face and pushing me into the bushes, where there were two men with their trousers down. Both had erections.

Getting onto my knees, I was forced to use both my hands on the men at the same time. I could feel tears welling up but I was defiant – not letting them fall. I remember seeing old condoms scattered everywhere on the ground.

'You're so sexy, I heard you give good hand and blow jobs,' one of them muttered over and over as I almost gagged.

Soon, the rapes at the dogging sites began to meld together and played like a disjointed movie reel in my head. I blocked out a lot of what happened, but I did recall snatches of different incidents, sometimes several on the same night. They were seared into my mind; I couldn't shake them, even from my dreams. Years later, memories can be triggered by the musky smell of a particular aftershave or a similar-looking man I see walking down the street.

One night, I was forced into the back of a van and raped by Grandad and a tall man with grey hair and saggy skin who wore his wedding ring. Another time, I was in a silver Jeep with the car seats pushed down. A man fondled my bits and then I had to have sex with him. Then, there was a squat, grey, overweight man in a van. I had to give that one a blow job, while every inch of my body shuddered with disgust.

I remember one night I was crying, yet Grandad held me tightly and pulled my hair, saying I had to do it or he would give me a harsh punishment which wouldn't be nice at all. Then, I was pushed up against a tree and raped by him and violated by another man.

There were often queues of men outside Grandad's work van. On one evening, there were three waiting to get their grubby hands on me. The first one licked me between my legs while I sucked his willy. The second raped me and the third man, I had to pleasure with my hands. It felt endless. My dignity was in tatters.

One day, Grandad stopped me going to school. The summer sun poured through the windows and when Grandad said we were going to the seaside at Ingoldmells my heart leapt with relief. I thought: *Great, nothing bad is going to happen to me today. We're just going on a day trip.*

He took me to the market where he bought me a baby pink Playboy t-shirt, a powder blue one emblazoned with the Playboy bunny, a fake Nike Air hoodie and some of those Heelys, which were trainers with a wheel on the back. We tucked into fish and chips and Dunkin Donuts slathered with chocolate sauce and sprinkled with sugar. For those brief moments, I fooled myself into thinking I was just any other teenage girl out at the seaside with her grandad. Onlookers glancing at us laughing would never have guessed any different. On the way home, we pulled up into a huge layby so I could have a wee.

Afterwards, I was testing the Heely shoes. Only, I couldn't get the hang of them and I fell and cut my knees. But I didn't really care – I was laughing as it was so much fun to have these brand new things that everybody wanted. Grandad laughed at me and said I was a bloody idiot for wanting them. He thought it was funny that I couldn't use them.

When we got back in the car, the atmosphere quickly changed. Without a word, he shoved me onto the back seat, pushed my face up against the window and raped me from behind. It took my breath away because of how suddenly the attack had happened. It just came out of nowhere. One minute, we'd had this nice, normal day out and the next, he had ruined it. My whole body tensed up in shock. I sat quietly in the back until we were home. I was so traumatised at what had just happened, I couldn't even move …

I'd almost become used to the rapes but this felt as if it was the first time again. It was so much worse than some of the others because we'd been having such a nice time beforehand, just a girl and her Grandad at the seaside. What could be more carefree and comforting than that? So for him to force himself on me after I thought we'd been getting on so well came out of the blue and sent me reeling. I thought maybe he'd been feeling sorry for me, for what he was making me do. But was he just softening me up before striking?

Still feeling shaken a few days later, I was withdrawn at breakfast, giving Grandad just one-word answers.

'Cheer up Emma, I'm going to treat you today,' he smiled. He ushered me into the car and drove to McDonald's in Sleaford. It was on a roundabout off the bypass and when I saw the big yellow 'M', I couldn't help smiling.

I had a McDonald's breakfast with two bacon and egg McMuffin meals, a Coke and fresh orange juice. After I'd finished, Grandad handed me a plastic bag.

'Put this on and don't ask questions,' he said.

Inside were black stockings he had bought from a Co-op. I gulped, my throat constricted with fear. *Some treat*, I thought to myself, shivering. We got back into the car and a few minutes later, we pulled up at Sleaford train station. I was forced into the back seat. Suddenly, the door swung open and a man came out in crumpled work clothes and got in the back next to me. So that's what the slap-up Maccy D's meal had been – payment.

I froze. The stranger kept grabbing at my breasts.

'No, please,' I begged, but he still carried on.

We pulled up to a forest and Grandad made us walk into a clearing. He put his jacket on the ground and pushed me down to lie on it. The scruffy man climbed on top and had sex with me as my grandad stood over us, touching himself. I turned my head to the side and closed my eyes, praying it would stop and that I was dreaming.

When it was over, I couldn't get up. I felt so weak, broken and sick to my stomach. I didn't bleed very often now but I had a sharp soreness inside me. I couldn't fathom how these men could be turned on by violating a helpless, distressed young girl. A child. I came to realise that these men didn't want just sex. If they did, they could go to an adult prostitute. These men were after a young girl who they viewed as pure and innocent. And Grandad provided this black market for them. The sex was always rough and fast. They didn't care that they hurt me, tore me even, because they just wanted to get the goods they'd shelled out for.

My grandad got hold of my arms and pulled me up. I was bundled into the car next to my attacker, who kept sneering at me. After dropping the man back to his work, we arrived at the flat. Running to the bathroom, I locked myself in and cried so hard, I didn't think I'd ever stop. Next, I showered and scrubbed my skin until it was red raw.

But I couldn't get rid of the man. I kept smelling him on me and finding bits of tree in my hair. I was so itchy and sore. No one I knew had an inkling of this shady twilight world I'd been plunged into.

Some of my friends were getting boyfriends. With outrageous hypocrisy, Grandad told me that they were 'bad' and 'naughty' for going out with boys. I believed him. I thought it must be wrong.

Sally had a boyfriend, too. They hadn't done anything, only kissed. They'd go round to each other's houses and snuggle up to watch films. Some of the other girls had started sleeping with boys around this time. They'd brag about it at school, saying how good it felt.

Once, I went with a group of girls to buy the morning-after pill at a chemist's. I pretended to know what it was for but I didn't really have a clue. Even after everything I'd been exposed to, no one had ever given me a proper sex education. Because the girl was only 12, the pharmacist called the police and I scarpered. That made me believe Grandad even more – that having boyfriends meant you weren't a good girl. He'd twisted everything.

Meanwhile, I was finally allowed back into mainstream lessons for good behaviour and in time for the new school year, in September 2007. I felt as if I'd been released from prison.

My friend Beth and I were thrilled to be reunited again. We passed notes to each other, arranging to go up to the fields at lunch time to have a smoke. We'd also go swimming and to the cinema together. Beth had a long-term boyfriend now. I'd often hang out with them both. He was nice and polite and treated her well.

We were also studying for our SATs exams. I remember sweating with nerves in the exams, but I managed to sit my maths, science and English tests. One of my proudest achievements was managing to pass them even while I was in the midst of the abuse. How I did it, I'll never know.

At home, I managed to keep up the facade that everything was fine. Whenever I felt close to letting slip what was happening to me across the road, all it took was recalling the threatening glint in Grandad's eye that if I breathed a word no one would believe me, or I'd be taken away, my parents would be deeply ashamed of me and it would kill him, to keep my lips firmly sealed.

One night, my sister Lizzie was getting ready for a night out.

'Please can Emma come with us?' she begged Mum and Dad. 'We'll look after her.'

'Go on then, but just this once and don't stay out too late,' Mum said. 'She's only allowed lager. No spirits,' she said.

I couldn't believe it – my first night on the town. I was bubbling with excitement.

'I can do your hair and make-up – you'll look so pretty,' Lizzie smiled.

I watched myself transform from a young girl into a woman in the mirror as Lizzie applied foundation to my face, slicked on liner round my eyes and gave my lips a coat of coral pink lipstick. Then, she straightened my hair with her hot irons.

'You look beautiful,' Mum said, pulling me in for a hug. 'Be good,' she smiled.

After my sister flashed a fake ID for me, we tottered into the club. I felt all grown up in my new blue dress with little cap sleeves and high heels. Dancing to the music, I felt so free. Whenever a man came up to me, my sister took my hand and we walked away. She was very protective of me and didn't even let any of them talk to me. I was glad. I just wanted to soak it all up and get swept up in the music, lights and freedom. We left at midnight and got some chips with cheese and gravy from the chippie.

Mum and Dad were waiting up for us.

'Did you have a good night?' Mum asked.

'It was brilliant,' I chirped.

'Don't go making it a regular thing,' Dad said.

That night, I went to bed at Mum and Dad's, with a smile on my face for the first time in a very long time.

Although it felt as if things at school had settled down and I'd tried to keep my head down, one day trouble flared up once more.

One lunchtime, I'd gone to the field to have a cigarette. Suddenly, there was some jostling and someone pushed me into a boy.

'That's my boyfriend you just touched, you bitch,' a girl spun round and let rip at me.

'Shut your mouth!' I retaliated.

Fixing me with her beady eyes, she pursed her lips. 'Just because you can't get a shag off anyone but your dad,' she taunted.

What has she just said? Has she guessed my secret? Does everyone know?

I knew it was probably just a horrid coincidence – the worst insult she could think of to aim at me – but it was so close to the truth, it shook me to my core. I felt as if I was a pressure cooker about to blow. Shaking with rage, I grabbed her by the hair and head-butted her. I don't recollect much after that.

The next thing I remember was being marched to the headteacher's office, who told me the board of governors would have to be called in. I was suspended for a week and told they could expel me. As you can imagine, Mum and Dad were at their wits' end.

'We're so embarrassed by your behaviour,' Dad said.

'Your mum and I have been talking and if you get into any more trouble, I'll take you with me to Ireland to get away from everything. Start afresh.'

I absolutely hated the idea. It felt like a million miles away.

'I've got my friends here, and school,' I cried.

It was a scary prospect to be sent away from all that was familiar, especially for a teenage girl. It did cross my mind that I would be far away from Grandad, but he had this sickening hold over me. I didn't quite understand how strong or deep it went. Somehow, even if I was in another country, I believed I could never completely escape Grandad's clutches.

And even though it sounds crazy, I still loved my grandad. I knew that the abuse, the rapes, the pimping out to men at dogging sites, was wrong. It felt wrong and it had left me an empty shell of a person, but I just faithfully trusted what my grandad was telling me. That this was what happened between girls and their grandads and it was the price I had to pay to prove my love for him.

When he learnt about Dad's threat, Grandad was furious. 'You can't keep playing up at school,' he said. 'It'll ruin everything.' And that's when Grandad took his deviousness a step further.

A few days later, he went into school and told the head that my parents had left me in his care because they had moved to Ireland. But of course it was all a lie. A sick masterstroke. That meant he was my sole guardian. He changed the address and emergency number that the school had for me to his so that my parents wouldn't find out if I got into trouble again and couldn't take me away to Ireland.

I think he got a kick out of how clever he thought he'd been. After that he would make me play truant on a whim and know that the school would never call my parents. I thought no one could touch him – he was invincible and beyond the law. With such total and all-encompassing power over me, what would be my fate? What was next? Would I ever be free?

Chapter 7
Go and don't look back

By the spring of my fourteenth year, 2008, my life felt like one of those white-knuckle roller coasters at the fair. There would be the relentless abuse and then brief bursts of normality when I tried to catch my breath. Deep down, I thought this was how my life would always be. I was too intimidated by Grandad and the men to resist them. I blocked it out just so I could get through it. I couldn't visualise a way out. Every day when I woke up, either after a night of being pawed by disgusting old men in muddy laybys or mauled by my own grandad in his bed, I told myself, *You've got to toughen up, girl.* I built up an almost impenetrable shell to withstand the horrors I was experiencing. But inside, I was a quivering mass of insecurities, fear and despair.

At school – my only escape from Grandad's ever more frequent and brutal attacks – I desperately wanted to tell someone what I had endured for the past three years.

I still believed him on some level when he said what was happening to me was normal, but I was getting older, and becoming more rebellious and questioning. I dreaded and detested sleeping with sleazy strangers for cash with all my being and didn't understand why I had to keep on doing it when I didn't want to. Hadn't I proved my love for Grandad many times over? But I was still gripped by a mortal fear. Grandad had progressed to hitting me and slapping me across the face if he so much as sensed I was not willing to play the part of his compliant and dutiful sex slave anymore.

At school, I still constantly got embroiled in fights and was shut away in a room – in 'isolation' as it was called – in the hope I would change my ways. Never once did a teacher take me aside and show concern for my welfare. Instead, I was seen as the wild troublemaker who needed to be tamed. If only someone at the school had done their job properly and dug deeper into why I was lashing out, I might have received the help I was craving instead of being dealt punishment after punishment and treated as a hopeless tearaway.

Couldn't they recognise the vulnerable and beaten-down young child crying out for someone to understand her?

My poor parents were still completely clueless about the abuse being inflicted on their little girl. They thought my behavioural problems were down to hanging around with the wrong crowd, Beth and her friends, who were older than me and leading their impressionable teenager astray. They were exasperated and fretted about me continuously.

How could they have guessed that I was the victim of a paedophile ring who did unspeakable things to me at seedy sites around town? It was so preposterous, so unheard of. Yes, I'd heard of girls in other parts of the country in the care system falling into the hands of predators. But I was a well brought-up girl with a loving family. To my sadness, they never guessed the reason behind my outbursts. I didn't blame them, though. They trusted Grandad and I never let anything slip. It was school and the doctors I was angry at. They were supposedly trained to spot the signs but they failed me time and time again.

As well as making me feel low from the guilt and shame I experienced, the abuse was taking a physical toll on me, too. I suffered constant urine infections for which I saw the family GP. My private parts were inflamed, itchy, swollen and sore and I often had a smelly white discharge. I couldn't wee without it stinging. I was diagnosed with polycystic ovaries and an inflammation of the kidney. But even then, no one picked up the underlying cause.

When I was put into isolation at school after yet another misdemeanour, my grandad phoned up the school while I was there and said I was ill and unfit to attend. But on these occasions, they wouldn't let me go. I'd sigh with relief that I'd been spared a visit to the dogging site, but there was a heavy price I had to pay. My mobile buzzed with furious messages from Grandad saying it was my fault for messing up his plans and letting his clients down.

You're in big trouble he texted one day after failing to get me to bunk off. Wound up and terrified of what would await me when I got home, I threw a chair across the room at school and was given an extra day of isolation.

Letting myself into his flat after school as quietly as possible, I sneaked up to the bathroom and turned on the tap, the sound of the water helping to soothe my frayed nerves. I took off my school uniform and I slipped into the bubbles, closing my eyes and trying not to think about what his chilling words 'big trouble' could mean. But minutes later, I turned rigid with fright. There was a presence in the room. Peering out of the corner of my eye, I saw Grandad watching me as I bathed. I felt so weird and exposed. Of course, I'd realised Grandad loved watching me sleep with men almost as much as he liked doing things to me himself. He was a voyeur.

After I got out, I wrapped a towel around myself. But before I could get properly dry, Grandad, who was still stood watching me, suddenly lunged towards me. I stifled a scream as he lifted me up and carried me to the bedroom. Throwing me onto the bed, he growled, 'You'll be sorry, girl,' before raping me so forcefully I cried out in pain.

Throughout the attack, he stared out of the window in case my parents came up to the flat.

So that's how he taught me an unforgettable lesson for missing one of the visits to the men. A few days later, he pulled me out of school for the day and, this time, there was no way for me to dodge what was in store.

I knew the journey to the dogging sites Grandad favoured like the back of my hand now. Every bump, every turning made my stomach lurch in dread. I tried to zone out, to turn into a zombie so I wouldn't suffer the agony as sharply. But it didn't really help. It always made my soul ache.

When we got there, a tall sticky-palmed grey-haired man with a salt and pepper moustache was waiting in a layby.

I quickly realised that we had to follow him to a picnic place near Gainsborough, the scene of our tryst that night. Grandad led me to the man's car. Suddenly, my head was pushed onto his crotch.

'No, no,' I managed to yelp. But my hair was pulled and I was forced to suck the man's willy. It felt even worse this time because it was so sudden and I hadn't had a chance to psych myself up. I could hear Grandad's creepy laughter above me, saying how much he loved watching it.

A few months after Grandad had called the school and falsely claimed Mum and Dad had moved to Ireland, I had a row with my teacher. I told my dad about it – forgetting what Grandad had told me about not telling my parents about my bad behaviour – and he went to the school the next day. They informed him about Grandad frequently taking me out of school.

Furious, he banged on Grandad's door and shouted at him. 'You're not to go near that school again and don't you dare take Emma out of lessons,' he said. 'She is there to learn.'

He gave a snivelling apology and said I had called him to say I was sick. He never admitted what he had done. Dad told the school to make sure they never let me out when I was poorly and to call him and only him. But of course, that didn't happen.

A few weeks later, I was taken out of school during the day again, feigning sickness like Grandad had ordered me to. He picked me up in his work van and drove us to a chippie. We sat in silence and waited for random people to pull up beside us. Then, they followed us to a nearby park area. Grandad climbed out of the van and approached the vehicle, returning with a stranger in tow He opened the passenger door and this bloke stroked me up and down my leg and kissed my face to see if I was 'suitable'. I was still in my school uniform but this didn't make them flinch. In fact, it seemed to arouse them all the more. It was foul.

Grandad handed him the price list for me. That time, the man, who had deep-set wrinkles and looked even more ancient than the others, said he wouldn't be able to have full sex. But I wasn't spared. I was led down a little track into the bushes and had to perform a blow job on him, retching when he came into my mouth.

Once, on another occasion, I was with a man in the same bushes, stooped down in front of him on my knees while he started to undo his belt, when a dog walker came up to us and nearly caught us in the act. I froze.

A stream of frenzied thoughts swam through my head. *What will he do? Did he suspect? Will Grandad's cover finally be blown?*

Grandad's bellowing voice snapped me back to reality. 'She's looking for her favourite bracelet,' he said. 'We're helping her. She's sure she lost it when we came here for a picnic yesterday.'

The man with the dog nodded and smiled, seemingly satisfied with Grandad's made-up explanation. I was made to pretend I was looking for my bracelet until he left. Then we went back to his Cathedral City work van. Even now, when I see a van with that logo, I freeze.

Inside, Grandad passed me sex toys – the dolphin one and a love egg. I was forced to put the egg inside me while he pushed the dolphin up my bum. I remember I focused on sound of the rain splashing on the windows to numb the pain. When I tried to object and said no, he grabbed my head and pushed it up against the windscreen. Wrapping his clammy hands around my throat, his eyes bored into me. 'You have to do it, Emma,' he said. 'If not, I'll tell everyone what a slut you are and you'll be taken away.' My blood ran cold and my body turned limp as I let him have his way with me.

The lanes I spent most of my life in were muddy single-track roads with trees and bushes either side of them. Behind them, there were fields where you'd sometimes see, but mostly just hear, the low whirr from the tractors.

One time at the back of these lanes, a man in a glossy black, brand new BMW pulled up. 'Can I take her to mine later?' he asked Grandad. 'The wife will be out at work,' he smirked.

He looked to be in his fifties and wore a suit.

'Of course, whatever you want,' Grandad said.

But, thankfully, the man never came back.

That would be my last encounter for some time. And what led to my life changing came after a ridiculous row about false nails …

At school one day, during morning break, one of my friends was fanning out her fingers, showing me the manicure she'd had done. Suddenly, a girl came up to us and glared at her nails.

'You bloody copycat,' she yelled. 'You've only gone and had the same design done.'

I watched as they bickered over the false nails.

'Stop arguing, it's pathetic,' I laughed, rolling my eyes. 'They're just nails.' I wanted them to realise how ridiculous they were being and defuse the heightened tensions. But suddenly, the girl turned to me and lamped me. I was so stunned, I didn't do anything. My parents' threat to send me to Ireland was in the forefront of my mind and it stopped me lashing out.

The bell rang for the end of break and I filed into my lesson. After only a few minutes, I was called into the head-teacher's office.

'Did you hit the girl?' she asked me.

'No, she smacked me,' I protested. I felt outraged at being blamed for something I didn't do. If there was one thing I wasn't, it was a liar. I was banking on the CCTV to clear me. But even though it did, it didn't stop my parents from being brought into school and making good on their promise. When I saw Mum, she broke down in tears.

In the car on the way home, all I could hear were her sobs. I felt resigned to my fate. Even though I hadn't been violent this time, I had still failed them by lashing out on other occasions. Back in the house, we sat down in the conservatory with mugs of hot tea.

'We're sick of you getting into trouble,' Mum said. 'We want you to break away from the people you're hanging around with. They're no good.'

'We want you to build a future for yourself, a new life and a fresh start,' Dad added.

I burst into tears, barely able to speak. 'I don't want to go, my friends are here. I don't know anyone over there,' I cried. To me, Ireland seemed far away, desolate and strange.

'We had warned you this would happen but you're still getting into scrapes,' Dad said. 'You're being led down the wrong path and we're worried about how you'll end up. So you've left us with no choice. You and I will go to Mayo and you'll be enrolled into a school there.'

He didn't tell me how long it would be for. Dad had just done up a house there, but Mum wouldn't be coming because of her job. And I would be leaving in just two days.

It was all happening so fast, I couldn't take it in. I didn't hate my parents because I knew they were doing this for my own good, not to spite me. But it was still frightening to have to up and leave. I felt panicked that my whole life was changing. I'd never dealt with change well. What would happen when I moved there? Would I lose everyone?

I ran out onto the estate and found Sally in the park. 'I'm leaving,' I wept, falling into her arms. 'Text me, ok?' She nodded, tears streaming down her cheeks.

On the day we were due to fly, I went to see Grandad.

I'd been avoiding him. I knew he'd be angry with me but I couldn't go without saying goodbye. I felt a jumble of mixed-up emotions. On the one hand, I'd be free of him and the abuse. But I still loved him. Our lives had been inextricably linked after the activities he'd dragged me into. The hold he had on me was powerful and I

didn't know if I could survive without him, or him without me. Strangely, I felt responsible for him. It probably
stemmed from when I'd stayed over to look after him
after his heart attack. And then the rapes had become a
ghastly routine.

I walked into the living room and Grandad looked up
from the TV. 'This is your fault for getting into mischief at
school again,' he said. Then, a look of sadness swept across
his face.

'I don't want to watch you leave,' he said. 'It'll be too
hard for me. You might not believe me but I really do love
you.' He sniffed, beckoning me over for a cuddle.

I walked out in a daze of confusion. I just couldn't
make sense of my feelings. I felt a physical ache when I
thought I wouldn't see my grandad, but I couldn't understand why. Why would I miss the monster that had raped
me and watched as other men did the same? It was horrible
to admit it but I would. He'd consumed such a huge part
of my life for the last three years. It felt as if a part of a limb
was being cleaved from me. I felt lost and didn't know what
my purpose was, how I'd get through my days without him
planning virtually every minute of them. But at the same
time, I felt a rush of euphoria and excitement. Could it
really be possible that he wouldn't get at me there, in the
wild and remote coast of Ireland, which felt like a world
away from the dingy alleys and murky woods of Lincoln?
It was surreal.

Back home, Dad ushered me towards the car.

'Bye Mum,' I said, flinging my arms around her. I realised with a searing stab of pain how much I would miss her and my family.

'You can come over any time you want to, love,' she said, with red-ringed eyes. 'This will be the best thing for you. It'll be a fresh start by the sea with no distractions. You can get good grades and make nice new friends.'

'I'm so sorry, Mummy,' I gulped, the tears out of control now. 'I love you.'

'Oh, I love you more than I can say,' she sobbed. 'Go and don't look back, sweetheart. Don't look back.'

Chapter 8

A world away

Sitting in my new bedroom in the bungalow slap bang in the middle of nowhere, I gazed out of the window at the expanse of silvery sky. It looked like a page in a travel magazine – all perfect views and dazzling landscapes. I gasped when I saw dolphins leap out of the choppy waves of the Atlantic Ocean, transfixed by their acrobatic display. They made love heart shapes with their tails as they arced out of the water.

Ireland was beautiful – the scenery took my breath away. The weather was shocking sometimes, but on those wet and wild days watching the elegant dancing dolphins swimming in the swirling sea while we huddled up inside more than made up for it.

It was a world away from land-locked Lincoln and my old life of shameful nightly visits to dimly lit alleyways and murky dirt tracks. I started to feel as if I could breathe easier for the first time in years. My asthma, which had got worse since Grandad's abuse had escalated, bothered me less in the fresh sea air.

The house had four spacious bedrooms, two with en-suites, and a main bathroom. It had a crazy amount of land all round it. Opposite was the rugged and mostly empty beach. The sea was rough and Dad warned me not to go near it because of the strong current.

'People have drowned out there, it's dangerous,' he told me gravely one evening when there'd been a power cut and we'd dined by candlelight. It scared the bejesus out of me.

We'd moved to a tiny town called Belmullet in County Mayo, on the west coast of Ireland. It was a wild and remote place made of trails, craggy coves and deserted beaches, with plenty of space to let off steam. It was so isolated, there was just one high street in the whole area, with a family-run butcher's, a florist and a hairdresser's. There were no motorways, bypasses or big Tescos. It was small-town Ireland with a population of 1,000 and it looked as if it had remained unchanged for decades.

Once the novelty had worn off though, my first few weeks felt endless and boring for a teenage girl. My days mainly consisted of sitting inside and watching TV shows. There was Jeremy Kyle in the morning, then from teatime a roll-call of the soaps: *Neighbours*, *Hollyoaks* and *EastEnders*. As it was already the summer holidays there, in June 2008, I didn't have school to keep me occupied. Dad and I would go for bracing walks down to the beach to 'keep fit', as he said. I was excited as Mum was coming over soon to visit. I knew Sally was allowed to stay for the summer, too, which was something to look forward to when the loneliness crept around my heart like tendrils of ivy.

I chose the en-suite room facing the beach, which was a beautiful and soothing sight to wake up to. My bedroom had a wall of built-in wardrobes. In the middle was a dressing table with a big mirror. It was white and so pretty, with swirly roses decorating the frame.

But I missed my friends in England terribly and still struggled to escape Grandad's grip, even here. Because Dad banned me from smoking, I sneaked roll-ups from Mum before I left, smoking them in my en-suite, spraying deodorant and brushing my teeth afterwards to hide the smell. Once, I found three packs of fags tucked inside the back of the wardrobes, which thrilled me – it was like Christmas had come early. I couldn't completely let go of my old life and Grandad's influence.

At dinner time, Dad made fry-ups. The bacon was so thick, freshly cut by the local butcher. We also had boxty, a fluffy potato pancake and an Irish favourite. I didn't usually like sausages but I liked the Irish ones.

As I settled into this new and exotic place, far away from Grandad, I felt calm and peaceful. I was getting along with Dad really well. I think he felt sorry for me missing my friends.

'I've brought you here because I care and love you,' he said softly when he caught me scrolling through old photos of family and friends on my phone. 'I want the best for your future, and the people you were with were no good for you.'

He was referring to the school bullies but little did he know who else those words applied to. Maybe Dad was right. Perhaps in this wild and mysterious land, separated from my tormentor by swathes of ocean, I'd finally be safe.

As summer continued, my relationship with my parents grew stronger. When Mum came over we went for walks and had meals out and it was amazing. I realised how much I'd missed them. She left in October, a week before my niece – Lizzie's daughter – was born. I missed her like mad, but we spoke on the phone every day.

I was of course relieved I didn't have to keep doing what Grandad had been making me, but flights were very frequent, which meant we could often go back. Shortly before our first trip back home, I got a parcel. Excitedly, I ran up to my room and ripped open the paper. A mobile phone tumbled out, along with a folded-up note. It was from Grandad. My pulse quickened and I held my breath as I read. *This phone is yours but you're not to tell your dad about it*, he had written. *I will top it up and send the code through so you and I can have secret conversations away from the landline in the living room. Love Grandad.*

A bolt of terror flashed through me. Even though he was in another country, I felt as if he was always here and, now, with this phone, he could keep tabs on me.

When the mobile buzzed, I almost dropped it in panic.

'Hello?' I squeaked, even though I knew it was him.

'Hello Grandad's girl,' he said. 'It's so good to hear your voice. I'm missing you very much.'

My mind whirling, I mumbled something about missing him, too – I didn't know what else to say. The truth was, I wasn't missing him at all. Suddenly, his cheery tone switched.

'I need you to stay quiet because if you breathe a word, you will never be allowed back to England to see your friends and family again,' Grandad warned.

I felt so scared and distraught at the thought of never seeing them again that I agreed not to say anything and hid the illicit phone in my wardrobe, buried deep under some clothes.

When Grandad called the next time, he told me he had a girlfriend called Paula but that I was, and always would be, his number one girl. I'd seen her around in the past and thought she was just a mate. But hearing he had a girlfriend his age made me feel both strange and relieved at the same time. Part of me thought he'd spare me now, but another part felt inexplicably jealous. When he referred to her as a 'slag', it made me wonder if she was a bad person and if Grandad really liked her.

Soon, it was time to fly home for the visit. I was so excited to see my family and friends, but nervous about catching up with Grandad. Would he be how he used to be before the abuse? Maybe he'd missed me so much that he'd not hurt me anymore? And now he had a girlfriend, would he even need me? Or would he be worse than before because, in his mind, I'd messed up and got myself sent away?

After the 50-minute flight, I laid eyes on Grandad at the airport service garage, where he was waiting to pick us up. We walked towards him and he greeted me with a cuddle and kiss on the cheek.

'I've got you coffees,' he beamed.

He's doing his Mr Nice Guy act, I thought, telling myself not to get sucked in. He didn't speak to me much in the car, other than making small talk about how I was finding it, if I was looking forward to starting school and whether I had made any friends. Then he had a chat with Dad and they shared a few jokes.

I stayed at Grandad's while I was there for a few days. Grandad offered and I knew I had no choice as that's the way it had always been. Refusing would have raised eyebrows from Mum and Dad and they'd have questioned me – exactly what Grandad had warned me to avoid.

I went to the social club with him and Paula on Sunday in the day for a few hours. We ate lunch and he bought me alcohol and cigarettes, so I could smoke and drink with them. It made me feel all sophisticated and grown-up. I'd forgotten how delicious that sense of being treated as an adult was. I left early and he stayed on with his girlfriend. *Maybe this is how it will be with me and Grandad now*, I hoped. But the next night, when I climbed into bed, Grandad lunged at me. Paula never stayed over – Grandad stayed at hers some nights but was often at his flat, especially as I was back for a visit. And of course, I knew why. Virtually as soon as we were alone, he had his arms all over me and started giving me slobbery kisses.

Next, he pinned me down and forced himself inside me. I felt numb and cursed myself for believing that he'd leave me alone. Now I was a bit older and had had some distance from him, I started to feel really emotional and confused as to why he would do it if he loved me and it hurt me. I'd got used to it not happening, but now I had to go back to keeping secrets.

I knew I was safe from Grandad in Ireland. I knew he would never set foot there because he was a racist. Although he never showed it to my dad, he would rant to me about the IRA. So it was a relief when, a few days later, Dad and I went back to Ireland by boat. Sally came with us, too, and it was so good to see her and spend time together.

The journey took over eight hours, and we sneaked out onto the deck of the ferry and smoked, laughing about people we knew. We got breakfast and dinner in the evening – it felt like an adventure. We shared a room with two beds and chatted long into the night about what we would do when we got to Ireland, like going to the beach and the teenage disco in the town.

The first thing we did was go swimming at the leisure centre. We walked the five miles home, but it felt like a flash because we were giggling and talking non-stop. I was happy she was there – it was so much fun having my old friend in such unfamiliar surroundings, and it was a wrench when she left a few weeks later.

'Don't forget me, do you promise?' I sobbed as I threw my arms around her.

Soon, the summer holidays came to an end and I started school. I was keen to make a fresh start and I flourished. My funny, feisty personality, no longer stifled by Grandad or the bullies, came to the fore and I made lots of friends. We went to the back of an old building with no roof, where we smoked and played football. Smoking was normal for me by this point so it just felt right to continue. I got stressed in lessons having to go without one, so I went to the toilet in between lessons and lit up. My new friends and I texted all the time and met up in town after school to go to the pier and just mess around, jumping onto the boats. We also hung out at the disco, which was like a nightclub for under 18s. We sneaked alcohol in past the bouncers and danced and gossiped. They were all older as I was put in the year above.

My relationship with my parents continued to improve. We talked more, and it hit me that even though I'd been seeing them in England, I'd been missing them at the same time because I felt I couldn't really talk to them. But here, free from Grandad's watchful gaze, I could be myself. I'd laugh and joke with them and I felt as if I was being more open because I didn't have to pretend, or lie about what I'd done that day to keep my encounters with Grandad and the men a secret.

Dad agreed to buy me a puppy from a friend of his – a sweet and energetic Border collie I named Lassie. I went to the beach alone and walked her, before sitting on the rocks and watching the sea. Staring at the ebb and flow of the sea calmed me down and was like therapy. All the hiking, too, made me tired and I slept deeply. Looking out of my window towards the ocean also helped comfort me. I just watched it, blocking out everything else.

A couple of months passed and Dad and I were due to go back home later in the week for half term. My second visit elicited a mixture of emotions inside me. Delight at being reunited with family and friends but sheer dread at being under Grandad's control again.

The day before we flew, to give me a send-off, my friends and I organised a trip to the beach after school, where we threw a going-away party. One of my mates, Andy, smuggled bottles of vodka, whisky, beer and wine down there and we knocked them back for hours into the night.

Somehow we stumbled into school the next morning and went to our first lesson. But when we realised that we could barely stand, we sneaked back to the rocky beach to sober up, skipping the rest of our lessons. Only, to our horror, the head and the gym teacher caught us. We tried to run away and I fell off a rock, screaming as I plunged into the icy black sea. The headteacher dragged me out, coughing and spluttering disgusting salty seawater. I was soaked through, my teeth chattering and in a state of shock.

I didn't realise until it was too late what was happening as I was so drunk, but they frogmarched us into school and I knew we were in serious trouble. Then, watching as if a reel of film was playing in front of me, I saw Dad walk into school, and suddenly remembered he was coming in to tell them I wouldn't be in for a couple of weeks after the end of half-term. He was ushered into the head's office, where the headteacher told him everything I'd done – the drinking, skipping lessons and falling into the sea. I was suspended.

'I'm so angry and disappointed in you, Emma,' he scolded. 'How could you do this again? I thought you were getting on so well.'

He drove me home in total silence. He couldn't even bring himself to look at me, let alone speak to me. When we got to the bungalow, he ordered me straight to my room. I wasn't allowed out apart from to eat or go to the bathroom. I was barred from using the computer and I definitely wasn't allowed to go to England with him.

When I woke up the next morning, he had already left. He'd asked a friend to stay with me. Feeling lonelier than ever in an empty house, I felt so disappointed with myself for being so reckless, and seeing how angry my family was hurt me deeply. I had one serious hangover and kept throwing up. I felt so weak from all the drinking. I vowed I'd avoid it from now on.

When Dad came back a few days later, I apologised and he forgave me. He put it down to me adjusting to living in a new place and having to start from scratch. I'm not entirely sure if it was that, or if I was trying to get out of facing Grandad, but I was grateful that we could put it behind us.

When we went home for Christmas we went to my older sister Belinda's house, where I danced to Mariah Carey, stuffed myself with festive food and pretended we were a normal, happy family.

But it was the calm before the storm. I couldn't ignore the growing sense of impending doom building up around me.

Chapter 9

Crime scene

Come January, the weather in Ireland was so treacherous that my big puffer jacket, gloves and bobble hat were no match for the bone-chilling cold. The frozen landscape mirrored the icy shards of loneliness that stabbed my heart. So when my Auntie Susie and Gran Ellie came to stay for a few weeks, they were a welcome distraction from both the wintry weather and my increasing isolation. I eagerly lapped up even the tiniest snippets of the news from home, as if wiping my plate clean of every morsel, catching up on what I had missed with my family since I'd been gone.

Sadly, Sally and I had started to grow distant. She seemed so innocent and child-like, we couldn't relate to each other. And being so far away in Ireland made things even more difficult. I felt sad about it but tried to distract myself. Instead, Beth – the older, cooler girl from my old school – replaced her as my best friend. Even though I didn't see her that often, I felt we were kindred spirits because she seemed more worldly.

A few days into their visit, we got a call from my sister Lizzie and Uncle Tom. My grandad's flat was a crime scene.

He'd been arrested and nobody was allowed to set foot in his home. That was all we knew. Any other information was frustratingly scarce.

Eventually, the drip-drip of details began to emerge – each new revelation tightening the screw. To my horror, he had tried to commit suicide and had been admitted to hospital.

'Oh God, no!' I gasped, hands flying to my mouth. In that instant, I was 11 again and had just been told by my sister he'd had a heart attack. Those feelings of fear bubbled back to the surface. I listened in stunned silence as I was told he'd driven to a remote country lane and attached a hose pipe to his fuel tank and put it through the car window. As my nan and auntie recounted this to me, unable to hide their own distress and disbelief, I struggled to take it in or make sense of it. And the bombshells just kept on coming. He had been arrested on suspicion of the rape of two teenage girls, aged 15 and 16.

There was that harsh and brutal word, 'rape', again. It sent a jolt of fright through me. But it also produced a ripple of another sensation inside me: jealousy. I didn't want to acknowledge it, but it was there. What Grandad did to me hurt and confused me, but it was how he showed me love, how he proved to me I was special. If he had done the same to two other girls, was I no longer Grandad's girl? Didn't he love me anymore? My heart thudded in panic.

'The police said he arranged to meet them at Tesco,' Nan said as my mind whirled. 'He picked them up and drove them back to his flat and gave them vodka and lemonade, got them drunk and tried it on with them,' she said, shaking her head. 'It's sickening, they must have got it wrong.'

Vodka and lemonade. That was exactly what he gave me before he undressed me, rubbed his hands all over me and I became his toy. I couldn't think straight. I felt like my world had been turned upside down. I didn't know what to think or believe. Why would he try to kill himself and put us through all that pain? My nan and auntie were shocked and angry. They didn't believe it. They thought the police had made a mistake and that Grandad had tried to commit suicide because he was innocent. I had questions which I kept to myself for now – why had the girls accused him? Why were they in his flat? And why did he hurt us by trying to die?

Suddenly, Nan came to sit beside me on the sofa and turned to me, her eyes wide with concern. 'Love, I have to ask you this and you know that, whatever you say, I will believe you. Did he try anything with you?' she pressed gently.

After years of fear and control from Grandad, and now this latest horrible twist, there was only ever going to be one reply that could escape from my lips.

'No, never Nan,' I said, decisively. I denied it because he had just tried to take his life. If I admitted it all, wasn't there a risk he could try to top himself again, and this time succeed? No, I couldn't deal with having that on my conscience. I felt as if I was being tortured, my emotions being squeezed through the wringer.

My head spun as I tried to take everything in. I remembered a little red robin I'd seen in the morning, a few minutes before the phone call had come through. It had been hopping frantically on the ledge and peering through the window pane, as if it was trying to deliver an important message to me. Suddenly, it struck me why the sight of the bird had unsettled me. In my family, a robin always represents bad luck, a portent of doom. Either it would precede a loved one passing away or urgently contacting you to bring you some sort of warning …

I shivered uncontrollably but it wasn't from the winter cold. I couldn't process why this was happening. Had he tried to kill himself because of me, and what we'd been doing? Was this a sign of admitting what we had been doing was wrong? And what about the two girls – had he attacked them because I wasn't readily available anymore, or had he gone off me? Or maybe was it all some sort of terrible mistake?

After a day holed up in my room scared, shocked, anxiety-stricken and in disbelief, I decided to call him. I needed answers. I couldn't stop myself hyperventilating as I dialled his number on the mobile he'd sent me.

'Grandad, why did you try to die and leave us all? How could you leave me? Is it true?' I babbled, blurting everything out.

'No, it's all lies, don't believe everything you hear, my love. People have just got it in for me,' he said.

'And the girls? Did you …touch them?' I asked, holding my breath.

'Of course not,' he denied. 'I wouldn't do that, Emma. You know it's only you I love and always will be.'

But it didn't ease my mind. Switching on the computer, I typed in 'rape'. As I scanned the words that flashed up on the screen, I felt terrified. What they were describing was disgusting, violent and evil. Surely this wasn't the same thing Grandad had been doing to me for all these years?

A couple of weeks passed and my family and I were all still in a daze of disbelief. I got the blame somehow as false rumours flew.

'Are the girls your friends?' Paula asked. 'They could have set him up, and you would know.'

But that was not true at all – I had no idea who they were.

We were worried as Grandad had been sectioned and wouldn't speak to anyone. My mum had travelled over to the hospital two days after the news and he wouldn't open up. She was so angry. She wanted to know why the girls were round his flat and how he came into contact with them, but she was just met with a blank stare and a terse, 'Keep out of it.'

When I arrived back in England a couple of weeks later, I was still upset and confused. I'd researched rape further, and I couldn't process what I'd read. I couldn't stand it.

'Grandad, you need to tell me the truth,' I began, pulling up a chair at his kitchen table. 'Did you rape the girls?'

'No!' he said forcefully. 'The truth is, I was lonely and drunk and paid the girls to touch each other, as if they were lesbians,' he said. 'But they got hammered on my vodka, the silly girls, and stole £40 and accused me of rape.' He broke down in tears as he told me, which made me feel sorry for him and, finally, I believed him. Putting my arms around him, I gave him a cuddle.

I think I wanted to believe him more than anything. I wanted to believe the charges weren't true because of the seriousness of them.

'Everything will be alright, Grandad,' I said. 'You still love me, don't you?'

'Yes I do, you're Grandad's girl,' he said, stroking my hair. 'It hurts me to think of everything that's happened. It's because I missed you so much.' Guilt coursed through me and made me blame myself. 'You're the only one that can help me, Emma,' he said.

My feelings were in so much turmoil, the guilt a weighty burden on my heart, I began to try and distance myself from Grandad by spending more time drinking with my friends and not returning his texts or calls. But he made me feel bad by telling me he needed me, and that he could only get better with my help.

Whenever I came back to his flat on a visit from Ireland, Grandad had sex with me and took me to be abused by the men. I felt used and disgusting. But even though he couldn't physically touch me once I returned to Ireland, I couldn't completely shake him off. He texted me and called me to say how much he missed and loved me. He'd say how annoyed he was that I wasn't there and got upset with me, telling me that if I'd behaved myself, I wouldn't have been sent away. He got angry if I didn't reply to his messages quickly enough, so I always felt jumpy when his texts came through.

It was no good – I was caught in his grip.

A few months later, the charges were dropped by the CPS. Grandad was relieved and told me it was because the girls had bad backgrounds and were liars.

Back in Ireland, I began to get bullied again. I was texted messages by some of the girls from school saying I'd end up in a wheelchair because I was English. I couldn't believe the very thing I had tried to escape from was happening again. It seemed so unfair.

One day, six of them hung around after school and pounced on me as I walked out of the gates. They pulled my hair and tried to kick me, calling me 'English scum'.

A fierce swell of anger rose within me and I fought back, pulling two of the girls' hair and knocking their heads together. I pushed another who tried to put chewing gum in my fringe. I felt wild and out of control again and was so grateful I could leave for the summer, even though I was anxious about seeing Grandad again.

I was honest with my parents about the bullying in Ireland and they supported me and told me to stand up for myself. They'd noticed a distinct improvement in my appearance and attitude since I'd moved away. Despite the bullying, I'd made a couple of friends and even enjoyed some lessons again. I'd been less volatile and moody.

When I came home for the summer holidays in June 2009, I was so happy to see my friend Beth again. I was staying with Grandad but avoided him as much as I could by staying out with friends or seeing Mum and Dad. 'I've missed you so much,' I cried, wrapping my arms around her. 'I'm looking forward to going shopping and just having some fun,' I smiled.

I was in town with her one day and she'd brought a friend from school, Darren. 'There's someone I want you to meet,' she winked.

We clicked instantly, I just felt he understood me – quirks and all – and didn't judge. He made me roar with laughter.

We got to know each other over the next few days. He texted me funny and cute messages with lots of kisses at the end. I met him after he finished school – Ireland broke up earlier than English schools – and often I'd go to his for tea. His parents were so kind, making me feel part of the family.

Darren was as sweet as chocolate chip muffins and smelt like Lynx. He loved football and was going to get a scholarship in America. He had dark, wavy hair and wore braces, which gave him a touch of geeky vulnerability. He was so sporty, and when he wasn't on the pitch he hung out in the boxing gym.

As we spent more and more time together, I felt sad because I knew I had to go back to Ireland when term started. He was my best friend but over those heady weeks, something bloomed in my heart, the promise of something more than just friendship.

'I promise I'll get my parents to agree for me to come home for good,' I vowed.

'You better,' he smiled, hugging me.

***

At school in Ireland that autumn, I missed Darren like crazy. We confided in each other about problems at school. We supported each other a lot and talked every day on MSN messenger and by text. Whenever I came back to England we'd have such a good time going to the cinema, into town, meeting up with Beth, having dinner and play fighting. Then I would have to leave for Ireland and I'd get a sinking feeling in my gut. I hated it.

When I couldn't take it any longer, I spoke with my parents and begged them to let me stay and go to college at home. I told them about Darren and they took it surprisingly well. They'd known we were friends but I wanted them to know he meant more to me now and was worth getting to know better.

'I can see you're growing up and he's obviously a good influence on you if you want to go to college,' Dad said.

Eventually, I wore them down and they agreed, although they were upset that I was defying their original plan for me and were in two minds as to whether it was for the best. Reluctantly, I went back to Ireland one last time to get all my things, keeping my head down and counting down the days until I came back on the boat.

I felt so excited about seeing Darren again. I spent all my spare time with him – we would go to the cinema and swim at the leisure centre, giggling as we splashed each other. In September 2010 I started going college in order to complete my GCSEs. I didn't see Grandad as often because of studying, plus he'd moved from his flat to a house he shared with Paula.

One winter's afternoon two weeks before Christmas, as we stood outside a gorgeous old building by the castle, called the Lawn, Darren glanced at me shyly and fidgeted with the zip on his coat. Butterflies danced in my tummy.

'Will you go out with me, Emma?' he asked.

I blushed and felt as if I would burst with happiness. 'Yes I will,' I beamed. 'You make me so happy and I just always laugh around you.'

He placed his hand tenderly around my waist and pulled me towards him. As our lips met for the first time and we kissed, it made me feel smiley and warm inside. I couldn't even feel the sub-zero chill anymore.

Everything felt so right and, aged 16, I was head over heels for the first time. He was my first real boyfriend and my first proper love. Our relationship was all happy, carefree and jokey. He was loving and caring and we spoke all the time. I loved the feeling of contentedness and security he gave me and I wanted to spend every spare minute with him.

But I knew I couldn't tell Grandad about Darren, and I still couldn't escape his clutches. One day, he drove to my parents' house and demanded I sneak out some of my knickers to give to him. I shivered. It was so creepy and I felt shocked and confused at this new development. I tried to pass on washed ones, but he got angry and demanded my used ones. It was disgusting and humiliating. Another way for him to make me feel worthless.

He still arranged to see me alone, where he'd force himself onto me. He'd pretend to take me into town but then pull up at laybys and parks, and make me do horrible things with old, gross men, things I tried to block out, and then take their cash and watch furtively as they groped my shivering body. I remember thinking, *Why is this still happening?* The girls and the links to money would come to my mind and I'd wonder if I'd been told the truth. It hurt me even more because I wanted to spend time with Darren. I couldn't even text or call Darren when I was with Grandad because he'd get all possessive.

To be on the safe side, I changed Darren's name in my phone because once, when Grandad saw it flash up on the screen, he had flown into a jealous rage and hit me.

Strangely, I really liked Grandad's girlfriend Paula and we got on well. She would make me a coffee and we would chew the fat. One day, I confided in her about Darren.

'Please don't tell Grandad,' I quickly added.

'Why not?' she asked.

'He'll go mad and fall out with me,' I blushed.

'That's not on, I'll speak to him. It has nothing to do with him. You're growing up and it is part of growing up. You're not doing anything wrong,' she said. I felt a rush of warmth for her then.

She always asked me if I had spoken to Grandad. I hated to do it, but I felt forced to lie to her about Grandad texting me every day, keeping tabs on me. I had to pretend I hadn't heard from him because Grandad forbade me to breathe a word. He banged on about Paula being jealous and warned me she would get nasty if she found out. I couldn't understand it. It confused me.

But she soon cottoned on to the texts. I guessed she must have looked through his phone when he'd left it lying round. 'I don't care about him texting you, I just don't know why he lies to me about it. It's weird.'

I agreed but I kept tight-lipped. I realised Grandad's tactic was to try to turn us both against each other. 'She calls you a slag,' he told me constantly, which made me angry with her and not trust her, but then she would be nice to me and I wouldn't understand it. But Grandad kept drumming it into my head that Paula hated me, so eventually I started doubting myself.

Grandad never met Darren, but one night when I was walking with him, Grandad was driving around looking for me. He saw me and stopped by the side of the road, ordering me to get in his car.

I felt too weak to defy him. Grandad sped off, and once we'd got far enough away from home, he screeched to a halt. I was so frightened. Suddenly, he lunged at me and grabbed me by the throat. 'You can't be trusted,' he spat. 'You're dirty.'

He wanted me all to himself and didn't want me to get too close to anyone else.

'Get out,' he said, pushing me out of the car. I sat and sobbed on the roadside, crying for the little girl lost.

Darren knew my grandad disapproved of boys, which he was frustrated by, but I could never tell him the reason why. I used to say it was because he was over-protective of me.

I never, ever came close to spilling out the shameful truth. Not once. Grandad had trained me so well, and shame was the biggest silencer of them all. Why would I share something I felt so dirty and embarrassed about? I never wanted to tell anyone, least of all Darren.

Chapter 10
Awakening

The Sunday before Christmas, I tagged along reluctantly to the social club with Grandad and Paula. I would rather have been anywhere else, but it was tradition. We went every year and questions would have been asked if I'd tried to duck out of it. It was Grandad's favourite haunt and, that evening, he was full of festive cheer. I prayed it would be a good night and that maybe, as it was Christmas, he'd spare me.

Who was I kidding? A few minutes after arriving, I popped outside to smoke. It eased my creeping anxiety and, when I noticed a man next to me puffing on a cigarette, we got chatting and laughing. Suddenly, Grandad came blundering out like a raging bull and smacked the stranger around the face. 'How dare you try it on with my grand-daughter,' he fumed as he went to punch him again. 'She's only 16.'

I ran away in floods of tears, but he chased me, grabbed my hair and yanked my head backwards. 'I can't stand to see another man near you,' he said, shaking with rage. 'I hate the thought of it but I know I'm losing you,' he cried, crumpling over. I didn't know what to say or do. I hated that he always managed to make me feel pity for him, even after doing something horrendous.

Paula came running out looking horrified She'd been told he'd punched a man. She tried to defend me, and said it was strange he was acting like a possessive boyfriend. But as she attempted to calm him down, his anger boiled over again. Lashing out, he pushed her into the door and punched her. It was awful and I covered my eyes. No one else was around by then to witness it. I felt shocked and sad for her. I hated to see her hurt.

I know she'd begun to wonder why he lied about texting me and hid it from her. Then, his assault on the man who had tried to talk to me left her even more suspicious. And she'd faced his wrath herself. It was clear to me she was under his spell, too.

That night, I slunk home and crawled under my duvet to try and blot out the vicious events of that evening. I woke up early the next day with a heavy heart and couldn't stop thinking about Paula. I hoped she was ok. I wished she would escape him.

Then I remembered I'd arranged to go to Doncaster dome for swimming and ice skating with Darren. Instantly, my tense shoulders lowered. He had this magical ability to take my mind off everything and make all the bad things go away.

Christmas Day with my family was lovely, hectic, and yet uneventful. I gave Grandad a wide berth. He'd made me feel scared and horrible and I didn't want him ruining the day.

As the New Year approached, he kept contacting me and apologising. He begged for forgiveness and, eventually, I relented. I just couldn't see any other way around it. He had a way of pressing my buttons to make me feel so sorry for him, while also putting the fear of God into me at the same time. It was a toxic mix.

As Darren and I grew closer, I decided that I wanted to take our relationship to the next stage and sleep with him. It was something I'd been mulling over for a while, swinging wildly between feeling excited and scared. He'd hinted at it a few times, and I thought I was ready. But there was something I had to do, first. Knowing how smitten I was with him, when I told my parents I was thinking about it and could they take me to the doctor for an implant, they were surprisingly supportive. I'd been a bit nervous about telling them as we'd never openly talked about sex, but they seemed to respect that I was being sensible and responsible, and that I'd chosen to confide in them rather than sneak around behind their backs. I was relieved it hadn't been too awkward or difficult.

I knew about the risk of pregnancy by that point as I'd read about it when I'd looked up rape online after Grandad's arrest. It had been a lot to take in but my thoughts about sex being disgusting were being challenged by what I had discovered online. I learnt that intimacy in loving relationships helped you feel more connected to your partner. That, coupled with the fear of losing Darren if I didn't go ahead, is what made me decide I wanted to do it.

Mum and Dad used to let Darren come and see me and they'd grown close to him. One day, he joined us for a family day out to the beach. My happiest place was lying beside him on a soft bed of sand under blue skies. I was a normal, teenage girl on the outside, but inside I was battling my demons. Darren made me forget those temporarily and allowed me to feel good again.

A few days after the beach, Darren and I had been to the cinema and then caught the bus back to his place. We were in his bedroom listening to music and started rolling around and being playful. He started kissing me passionately and then he moved his hands over my breasts.

'If you're ready, we can take things to the next level,' he whispered. 'I love you, Emma.'

I froze and a sickening sense of realisation dawned on me. In that moment, I understood what had been happening to me – Grandad touching me in his bed, taking me to see all the men, forcing me to do sickening, unspeakable things. It shouldn't have been happening and it was all wrong. Darren had shown me that this should only happen in a loving, equal partnership, not be forced on a young girl.

I remembered how, when I told Grandad about schoolfriends having sex, he'd made an outraged face, saying they were very naughty and I shouldn't hang around with them. It was all one big lie. I should never have believed him. *They* were the normal ones.

It all just fell into place. My world came crashing down. It all made sense now – everything. It was like an awakening. The sordid secrets and lies of the last five years were in fact rape. I was being abused and sexually exploited by my grandad, who was trafficking me to seedy old men. I'd led a life no little girl should have been. My friends and family were the normal ones – not Grandad.

This blossoming teenage relationship had made me realise the depths of the degradation I'd been dragged into. In too deep, I felt too scared and ashamed to tell anyone about the rapes. I'd let them go on for so long because I was completely under Grandad's control, but I blamed myself for agreeing to sleep with him and the scores of men. How could I not be at fault if I hadn't said no? How could I not be tainted?

A torrent of emotions swept over me. I felt embarrassed, dirty, sad, stunned, naïve, disgusting and, above all, very stupid for believing him and allowing it. And then came another, horrifying thought. I didn't know how the hell I could get away.

I mumbled something about having to go back home and fled Darren's place. I ran and ran. Wildly, blindly, I raced down the pavements of my hometown, tears obscuring my vision. I stumbled and fell, but somehow I picked myself up and sped off like a missile whose target was the sanctuary of home.

I didn't notice if people were walking down the street. There could have been a gale blowing but I wouldn't have felt it. I was totally caught up in my nightmare and nothing else existed. When I reached my house, I was panting with exhaustion and my eyes were puffy and red.

'What's wrong with you?' Mum gasped, horrified.

'Oh, I'm just poorly. I think I'm coming down with something and just want my bed,' I babbled, staring at the floor and making a beeline for the stairs. I wasn't up to talking.

I could feel her concerned gaze boring into my back as I raced up, two steps at a time, and shut the door to my bedroom. Covering my head with the duvet, my tears were unstoppable. I couldn't wrap my head around the truth. Everything I'd believed was love was in fact monstrous. I felt frozen and sick.

Suddenly, my phone rang. It was Darren.

'What's wrong, you looked really upset and then you left in such a hurry?' he fretted. 'You looked as if you'd seen a ghost.'

'I'm just in trouble for not telling Grandad where I was, sorry for leaving like that,' I said, quickly coming up with a cover story. I felt eaten up with guilt and so I brushed over his questions by saying Grandad was angry with me. If I hadn't, I knew he'd just press me further and there was no way I had the words or the inclination to tell him my terrible secret.

Over the next few days, Darren kept contacting me to make sure I was ok. I was too ashamed to tell him what was really wrong, but I soon wanted to see him again. I needed him around – he was my best friend, first and foremost, the one I spoke to every day and shared almost every part of me.

But I couldn't stop thinking of my vile discovery – that what I'd thought was normal for the past five years was rape, abuse and a huge grooming process. He'd called me 'Grandad's girl', treated me to booze and cigarettes – and not because he thought I was grown-up and special, but because I would feel indebted to him and do everything he asked. It sent shockwaves through me.

A flurry of questions whipped round my mind like a violent storm. *Why is this happening to me? What have I done wrong to deserve it? How can I have been so stupid? Why does he want to hurt me?* Maybe I'd asked for it. I was old enough to know better. Surely I'd known it was unnatural to sleep with your own grandad but I'd gone ahead and done it anyway. I knew good girls didn't have sex, let alone oral and anal sex, with a man 50 years older, but I didn't stop it. Maybe I wanted the attention and it made me feel adored?

I felt so numb, I didn't know what to think or feel. I hated what Grandad made me do and I hated him for what he was doing to me. But I still loved him as he was still my grandad, the man I'd been closest to my whole life.

As time wore on, I started knowing, in my gut, that it wasn't my fault, yet still I couldn't break away from his grip. When he called me to come over to his or told me we were going to the alleys and carparks, I was paralysed with fear. I thought I would lose him if I refused or that he'd tell everyone it was all my fault and this disgusting secret would rip my loved ones' lives apart. Destroy them. So I talked myself into it.

Deep down, it was because I still loved him. I desperately didn't want to but those feelings ran deep and I wanted his validation. There was still that naïve 11-year-old, craving his affection and thinking he loved her so much after showering her with gifts and his undivided attention. He'd always tell me he loved me, that he'd protect me from everyone – from the bullies, the other men, from my overbearing parents. I couldn't just shut out the fact he was my grandad and, despite what he had done, I always saw the good in people. So I hated him for what he was doing but then I would remember who he was supposed to be. Only *he* understood me.

I never told my grandad that I had realised he'd raped me, as I was so scared of what would happen. I was fighting a losing battle.

One day I was poorly at college, and I didn't know who to call to take me home. I felt so sick, and the only one I knew who could collect me was Grandad. But instead of showing me sympathy, he drove me to the dogging site and forced me to walk down the lane. Leading me into the bushes, he said I had to touch a small, skinny man with greasy hair and glasses. I had to give him oral sex. I was so upset.

'But I'm ill, Grandad,' I pleaded.

'I don't care, it doesn't matter. You have to do it,' he said, callously. Afterwards I threw up. He drove me home in silence apart from my muffled sobs. I was crying because my head hurt so much with the burden of knowing what I knew.

One day, while Paula was at work, he raped me in the living room so he could see out the window in case anyone came. I felt isolated, lost, confused and dirty. I wanted to know what I had done to warrant this. I felt a surge of pain through my chest and a stab of anxiety.

Once, at a picnic place, he had arranged for me to crawl into the back of a small white van and he and the driver abused me at the same time. I tried to pull away and explain that I really didn't want to. But Grandad became angry and frustrated. I was so scared and sick to my stomach. The man was fat, grey-haired and grunted loudly, which made me feel even worse. I could feel his body hair on me and it felt like metal wires on my skin.

And on and on my secret, sordid life continued.

I felt as if I was going through the motions of living, that I was worthless. Darren was the only good thing I felt I had, but I couldn't understand why he wanted me. Couldn't he see I was unlovable? Dirty? Part of me was terrified he'd leave me.

We didn't sleep together for another two months. I just didn't feel ready. Sometimes I hated the thought of it, and tussled with it mentally because I had now realised the truth of what was happening with my grandad. I associated the act with feeling sick, angry and hurt.

I was trying to swallow the bombshell truth that Grandad did not love me at all and it was all part of his plan to hurt and abuse me. That made me begin to feel closer to Darren because he was honest and respectful. When he broached the subject of being intimate again, I didn't want to lose him. I began to read more about sex within a loving relationship, how it could be good and bring people closer.

Darren was so loving and kind. He never forced me to do anything, or made me feel pressured.

When it happened, it was just a normal day. We'd hung out together and were just in casual clothes. He had his joggers on and I was wearing a multi-coloured dress over leggings. I felt a bit of a mess to be honest.

As we started kissing and things became heated, my head raced. My thoughts were all over the place. I still felt I was being dirty and bad. But after we'd slept together, Darren was so affectionate and we lay together all sweaty and giggly, legs and arms entwined and cuddled for hours.

However, the reality hit me hard when it came to leaving that blissful bubble. I got tearful because of the conflicting emotions raging inside me. Darren tried to comfort me but he didn't understand. How could he when he didn't know? I also started my period, which made me feel embarrassed and as if I was being punished for doing it.

Meanwhile, I had no choice but to be at the beck and call of Grandad. His abuse was relentless. He would get angry and turn up whenever he wanted to. He'd started taking photos of me when I was being molested by the men and I'd open up the snaps he texted me and feel horrified and see flashbacks.

He also forced me to send him naked pictures of myself. He knew just how to threaten and manipulate me to do what he wanted. I tried to avoid him as much as I could but he would guilt-trip me and scream and shout. He could be violent and would grab me by the throat, yelling in my face.

Every time he forced me to those dogging sites, I would feel heartbroken, like a part of my soul had been stolen. One time, I couldn't take it anymore and I cried, 'I don't want to!' I think he knew then that I'd figured out this was warped and wrong. I went very silent, and he couldn't help but see that I was at breaking point and might tell someone.

'Nobody would believe you, you're a liar,' he spat. 'I wouldn't survive in prison anyway.'

Of course, it felt worse now I knew the truth. I felt like a slag. I felt angry, hurt and betrayed. I'd lie there frozen, not knowing what to do or how to stop it because who would believe me over him?

I also thought about Darren. I was hoping and praying the abuse would somehow be over soon and he and I could be together properly. Maybe we could get married, have a baby with his twinkly eyes and my golden hair and we'd go on holidays to Spain.

I felt like my heart had a tear running through it that nothing could heal.

Chapter 11

'I can't do this'

Following this awful awakening about my secret life, the sense of self-loathing and helplessness within me grew like a cancer. I couldn't fathom how I'd ever break away from Grandad's control, so I figured the only choice I had was to submit to him and the 'clients' he lined up for me.

Grandad arranged dogging site visits once or twice a week and molested me himself three or four times a week. Sometimes he'd join in with the men, other times he attacked me alone. But each time I was forced to touch a horrible old man's privates or Grandad violated me, it took a heavy toll on my mental state.

I hated myself for letting those men rape me but I had no idea how to stop it. A third of my life had been consumed by this murky netherworld. It was a sickening; I felt like a helpless, tormented hamster furiously pedalling inside a relentlessly spinning wheel. Grandad had well and truly trapped me by warning me my parents would be ashamed of what I'd done, and every day I was made to do ever more despicable and unthinkable things that would make it even more difficult to open up or for anyone to believe me.

The only way I knew how to cope was to become angry, withdrawn and numb. I'd lie in bed all day sometimes if I could, became tearful easily and would start arguments over little things. And there was an ever-present tightness and pain in my chest which made me catch my breath.

I relied on college and Darren as my means of escape from that world. At college, I made new friends who didn't know anything about me. I could reinvent myself as a confident, normal teenager whose only worries were whether or not she'd revised for her exams or had the latest trainers. After lessons, we went to Subway to get our bacon roll dinner and catch up on gossip. Out of all my subjects, I enjoyed my law GCSE the most. The debates were helpful and cathartic. I could unleash some of the pent-up anger inside me that built up daily and nobody would realise the real reason for my fury – they'd just think I was throwing myself into the work.

Meanwhile, I kept up my normal act with my family. I couldn't imagine the shame my parents would have felt had they had any inkling what was going on with their youngest, who they still thought of as their baby. That knowledge would shatter their lives. But it was only a matter of time until the rage I tried to keep a lid on would find another outlet.

After we slept together, Darren and I became inseparable. He was my sweet, strong sanctuary and I found myself grinning soppily whenever I saw his face. For our first Valentine's Day as a proper couple, he pulled out all the stops.

'Come over to mine later, I've got a surprise,' he told me.

I counted down the hours, butterflies flapping in my tummy as I applied my lip gloss and mascara. When teatime came round, I waved goodbye to Mum and Dad and raced round to his. I was so excited to see him. I felt so happy and in love, it was like I was floating.

'Wow, you did all this for me?' I whistled, impressed, as I took in the scene. He had set the dining room table with candles, wine glasses, beautiful plates and cutlery.

'Of course,' he said, taking me in his arms and kissing me. 'And I've made your favourite – paella with bacon,' he announced.

'You know how much I love anything with bacon,' I squealed, clapping my hands with delight.

He poured Shloer sparkling juice – 'We'll pretend it's wine,' he winked – and lit the candles.

He'd bought me a teddy, chocolates and a bouquet of red roses. He was wearing a smart shirt with cufflinks and I was wearing one of my most sophisticated dresses. I felt so special. It was the perfect evening.

We sat at opposite ends of the table and talked about what we both wanted in the future. He wanted to be a footballer, while I shared my dream of being a paediatric nurse. We both joked about having a big, white wedding, lots of children and sports cars. I didn't want the night to end.

We kissed and lay down on his bed, cuddling and listening to music. His hazel eyes focused on me.

'I've noticed something, Emma,' he smiled. 'Your gorgeous green eyes turn blue when you're poorly or in a mood,' he mused. No one but my mum and dad had noticed that before. We had sex again and it was really romantic.

Later, his parents, who had been out at a restaurant, came back and dropped me home and we texted all night about being in love and how happy we were.

A few days later, it was my seventeenth birthday. I popped over to Darren's house and he took me to the cinema, where he draped his arm around me and stole kisses during the lovey-dovey parts. Afterwards, we went into town to find my outfit for my night out with my sisters.

Slipping into a cobalt blue mini-dress which made me feel like Rihanna, I did a shy twirl in front of him.

'You look absolutely beautiful, baby,' he gushed, his eyes shining with pride. I felt amazing, buzzing from his compliment.

Only, as I was about to head out of my parents' house and go out with my sisters, Grandad suddenly came out of the front room and spotted me and glared at me as if I was something he'd scraped off his shoe.

'You look like a slut,' he hissed under his breath so no one could hear. 'You just want the attention of boys, especially that good-for-nothing Darren. That dress doesn't suit you.'

I knew he was angry because I was wearing a short dress and he was jealous of other men looking at me. I knew he hated Darren, too. I kept telling myself I looked great in the dress but he made me feel horrible. I tensed up and the earlier confidence boost I'd received was long-forgotten.

Mumbling an excuse to my sisters, I ran to the bathroom and threw up. I was coughing and hyperventilating. I felt so upset by Grandad's verbal battering. Afterwards, I danced until my feet bled, knocked back cocktails, texted Darren through the night and tried to have fun, but I ended up getting really drunk as I hadn't lined my stomach. I still couldn't shake off Grandad's insult.

Over the next few weeks, I spent as much time as possible with Darren. It was as if part of me knew we were on borrowed time and I clung on to every precious second. We'd go into town and look around the shops in the day and chill to music at his place, just the two of us, or with Beth, too.

I barely saw Sally now. Our lives had tapered off in different directions. I felt so much more grown-up, while she was still a child. It was sad but we didn't really have much to talk about anymore.

At Easter, Darren joined my family – apart from Grandad, who avoided get-togethers – on a trip to Skegness. My parents really liked him, which made me feel good. We went to the amusement arcade and went on all the rides, going on the Waltzer over and over again. Darren got sick but I felt alive. It was an amazing day.

A week later, we went out for a meal with my family. I felt so happy and grown-up that my parents liked him and accepted me having a boyfriend after how protective they'd been of me. They were finally loosening the apron strings. He was allowed to come over whenever I wanted him to. I relished this new freedom.

And yet, all the while, Grandad was pretending to take me to college but making a detour to the dimly lit dogging sites near the RAF base, in secluded picnic spots and wooded enclaves.

It was the same routine. Grandad flashed his lights and a man, or a succession, came to a halt. Then, either I'd lie on the floor in the strangers' vans or on the muddy ground and the men would peel off my clothes, climb on top of me and rape me, while Grandad stood and watched. I'd just lie there, or other times, Grandad would instruct me to suck their penis. Sometimes, once the man had had his fun, Grandad would take his turn and have sex with me.

I felt an overwhelming sense of helplessness. I shuddered with dread when their rough, hairy bodies touched mine and I'd try to cross my legs, but I couldn't fight them off. I'd been completely conditioned into doing Grandad's bidding. I just wanted to get it over with, not let them see my tears.

I hated these monsters in suits and overalls. Most had wedding rings on. It repulsed me that they cheated on their wives and I wondered about their children. I questioned why they would do this. They showed not even a flicker of remorse. I'd worked out I must have been raped by more than 200 of them. It was hard to keep track but that figure seemed near the mark.

By now, I'd been reading up about what was happening to me and had come across a new word, 'paedophile' – adults who had a sexual interest in children. I'd stared at the computer screen open-mouthed when I'd found this out. I realised all these men must be paedophiles, a ring of them, led by Grandad, and I was a child prostitute because he was selling me to them for sex. It shocked me, this revelation, but still, I was too intimidated to tell anyone. At moments, when I felt a spark of strength, I'd fantasise about going to the police, but I'd never go through with it. After all, Grandad hadn't got into trouble after those girls' accusations. I'd started believing he'd done it but he was above the law. Untouchable. I was convinced the police would never believe my word over his, so what was the point? I thought my parents would believe him, too.

Grandad still made me send naked photos. When I didn't, he turned up the day after and became angry. Dragging me into the car, he vented: 'I need those photos Emma, you don't understand what it does to me when you don't send them. I can't cope when I don't see you, so make sure you send them next time.'

I felt so dirty and degraded. I hated him and what he was doing but I felt stuck and scared.

Summer 2011 came round, and the long, hazy days I spent with Darren were glorious. We often went to Swanholme Lakes and nature reserve, which was formed by a series of flooded sand and gravel pits. We swam in them and afterwards would crack open a can of beer and have a picnic.

We'd bring a portable stereo so we could blare out some music, playfight and watch the sunset, our arms around each other's waists. I felt ecstatic and so in love whenever I looked at him. When I was with him, I forgot the rest of the world, forgot Grandad and those filthy men.

When it came to leaving, I'd feel this great sadness in my heart. I hated lying and deceiving Darren but I could think of no other way. I didn't want to lose him.

Only, Grandad didn't stop trying to meddle. I'd hidden the fact Darren was my boyfriend, but he hated it whenever he saw us together. Whenever Grandad saw us, I'd drop Darren's hand or walk a few paces ahead to try to throw him off the scent. But, understandably, my behaviour hurt and confused Darren, and he started to get annoyed by Grandad's overbearing presence.

'He's just over-protective of me, we used to live together,' I'd say by way of explanation. But I could tell he was driving a wedge between us.

As the year hurtled towards Christmas, the day of my sister Belinda's wedding loomed closer. It had been the first family wedding for years and I'd been so excited about being bridesmaid. I'd helped choose a dress – a satin, floaty sea-green gown that Mum said made my eyes pop and made me feel like a mermaid. I longed to feel glamorous, grown-up and happy, but most of all, I wanted to walk in with Darren by my side. I'd dreamt about marrying him and this was the closest we would get in a while. But one day, as I was excitedly chatting to Paula about how I was looking forward to arriving at the event on Darren's arm and how proud I felt to be his girl, Grandad walked in. I froze as he shot me a look, his eyes coal-black with fury.

'Paula, can you leave us for a while,' he said, more as an order than a request. She knew not to argue with him in this mood, and after giving me a reassuring pat on the arm, she fled the room.

'Grandad, I was just talking rubbish, I didn't mean anything by it, it was just girl talk,' I babbled.

But he cut me off. 'Stop lying,' he barked. 'If you bring that boy to the wedding, I'll smash his face in,' he threatened. 'You know I can't see you with anyone else.' Then he turned and stormed out, slamming the door and making me yelp in fright.

I couldn't stand that Grandad had so much say in my personal life. I knew he would seethe with jealousy over any boy who got close to me, but I was a teenage girl who should be allowed some freedom. Grandad was still getting a piece of me and I was fulfilling his orders by seeing all those men. Why couldn't he let me have this one thing for myself?

But the more I pondered over it, the more I came to the same conclusion. There was no way Darren could come to the wedding with me. I knew how volatile Grandad was. I couldn't risk him hurting the boy I loved. So, a few days before the wedding, my heart clattering like mad in my chest, I dialled Darren's number.

'Hi beautiful, what are you up to? Helping your sis prepare for the big day?' Darren said in his sing-song voice. It always made me tingle.

'Oh not today, I just missed you,' I said. Then, 'Actually, I did want to talk to you about something.'

'You know you can tell me anything, babe,' he replied.

My heart could have burst in that moment.

'It's just that you can't come to the wedding, I'm so sorry,' I blurted out.

Silence.

'Why?' he said, quietly. I could catch a hint of hurt.

'It's Grandad, you know what he's like,' I said, trying to make light of it. 'He doesn't like me dating, he thinks I'm too young. I thought it was best not to provoke him. You understand, don't you?' I said.

'Em, I can't do this anymore,' Darren said. He sounded pained and frustrated.

'No, don't say that!' I cried.

'He keeps such close tabs on you, we can hardly see each other anymore,' he said. 'Your grandad will always be there telling you what to do. I love you but it's over.'

With those words, my heart shattered into a million pieces.

Only, I didn't plead for him to change his mind or beg him to stay. Because deep down, I knew he was right. My grandad was always going to be an overbearing presence in my life. He'd never set me free.

So, I let Darren go. I wanted him to be happy.

I was devastated by the breakup. We had got so close and he'd been there for me. I felt as if I was losing my best friend, too. It hurt knowing I would never again feel his touch, the softness of his skin or hear the sound of his heartbeat. But I also knew I wasn't right for him because of the chaos and darkness in my life, and especially because of what my grandad was doing to me. In that moment, I hated Grandad so much more for making me lose Darren. He was my boyfriend, my first love. But not only that – he was my escape. And now he was gone, thanks to the control Grandad wielded over me. But I detested myself too. For not being able to stand up to him, for letting him be my puppet-master and for intimidating me.

Throughout the wedding, I tried to go through the motions and pasted on a smile, but when I thought no one was looking, I crumpled into tears. I told my family Darren and I had split but didn't go into details. Grandad always seemed to be there, taunting me and giving me dirty looks. 'So he didn't come? Good,' he sneered. 'I can't believe you were going to bring him. You're a slag.'

Hasn't he done enough damage? Does he need to gloat about it, too? It was pathetic.

Afterwards, I went into town, sank vodka by the bottle and got blind drunk.

Grandad had won again.

Chapter 12
The only way out

Over Christmas and New Year, still nursing a broken heart, a rising sense of injustice at my situation flared up inside me. I'd lost every shred of my dignity, my innocence and now my first love – all because of Grandad.

Somehow, I survived the festivities – partly by drowning my sadness in champagne. My family's relatively tame dramas provided a welcome distraction. However much I'd grown distant from them over the last few years, and despite their struggles to understand my behaviour, with them I could pretend I was that feisty little girl again, not the tainted, feral slag I believed I'd become. And because he was spending Christmas at Paula's, I didn't have to cross paths with Grandad for a while so I felt I could breathe easier.

I started drinking more often after that Christmas; it became a way to blot out the pain and dull the righteous anger raging through my body. Vodka and other spirits were my poison. The hard stuff. It never failed to send me to oblivion. I had started looking unkempt, with straggly hair and I had a yellow tinge to my skin. But it made not a jot of difference to my insatiable abusers. Grandad kept hounding me to go to the dogging sites and raped me almost daily; it felt relentless.

So when I was booked in for a laparoscopy – an operation to treat my polycystic ovaries – in hospital I was strangely excited. It would be a respite from the constant abuse. No one could get their grubby hands on me in here. The doctors and nurses were my guardian angels.

Waking up in recovery a couple of hours after the procedure, still groggy from the anaesthetic, I peered down at the bandages swathed across my tummy and blurted out: 'Have you given me a tummy tuck?' I made everyone laugh with that wisecrack!

I felt so safe at the hospital and the nurses were kind and protective. It became a soothing haven from everything scary going on in the outside world. My grandad couldn't hurt me here, he couldn't drag me to those godforsaken places and pimp me out to the men. But eventually, it was time to leave. I heard Grandad's heavy footsteps on the tiles before I saw him and turned rigid in fear. He and Mum had come to the hospital to collect me.

Reality hit me hard then and I started formulating a plan in my mind to get myself back into hospital. What if I pretended to be sick, as a result of the op? They'd have to readmit me then …

So the next day, I stuffed myself full of crisps, chocolate bars and cake and made myself throw them all up in the toilet. Mum was so worried when she heard me vomiting that she promptly rushed me back to hospital. Secretly, I was ecstatic. It had worked. I'd covered it up so well. Nobody had cottoned on.

The doctors examined me but seemed baffled. They couldn't understand what was wrong with me. I realised the act of making myself sick gave me a strange sense of power. I couldn't control when my grandad hurt me but I *could* control when I hurt myself.

For nine weeks I managed to carry on the facade, making myself vomit and using the op as an excuse to prove to the hospital, to my family, that I was genuinely ill. It relieved some of the pressure of what was happening to me. The control I regained was a coping mechanism. I felt a thrill from it. It was addictive.

My frantic parents visited every day. They were so worried – my weight had dropped considerably and I looked like a bag of bones. They demanded the hospital keep doing checks. They were convinced I was poorly because of the surgery. I couldn't help feeling guilty for making them fret, but the lie just spiralled. My need to stay in hospital was too great.

I had another regular visitor. Grandad. He would creep in when Paula was at work and bring food, fags and money, acting like the model grandparent. *Maybe he does care*, I thought, but little did I know it was a debt …

Eventually, after exhausting every possibility, the doctors decided my symptoms were psychological and suggested counselling. I knew then I couldn't keep this act up so I fixed a smile on my face and told my family I felt better.

'You can go home,' the doctor said cheerily. My heart sank.

On my last day in hospital, Grandad came to see me, waiting until the nurses were out of earshot to issue his demand.

'I've given you all this money and you haven't given me anything,' he snarled. 'You need to do what I want as soon as you are out.' Of course, I knew what he meant.

My chest tightened and I felt as if I was having a panic attack. When he left, I started crying hysterically. I no longer felt safe there. I told the nurses I was upset because of the pain and they gave me morphine, which plunged me into a disturbed, nightmare-filled sleep.

Back at home, the urge to make myself sick didn't leave me. It became a compulsion. I stuck my fingers down my throat up to four times a day. I avoided eating but when I had no choice but to eat meals in front of my family, I'd secretly throw it back up in the bathroom. I didn't realise it but I was in the grip of an eating disorder. I found strength in it when I felt weak at most other times. My mind was becoming more scrambled by the day.

I couldn't deal with what was happening to me anymore. I felt so helpless and vulnerable. As soon as I left the hospital I knew I was no longer safe from Grandad's clutches. I knew he was always going to be there, like a menacing shadow. I felt stuck and so sad and I was convinced there was no way out of this hell as he had drummed it into my head that nobody would believe me.

That's how I came to believe there was only one option. *Ending it all.* With trembling hands, I popped paracetamol tablets into my mouth as if they were Haribo sweets. I was crying with each one I swallowed.

This is the only way out, I repeated to myself, trying to block out images of my family that flashed into my mind. I could not escape my grandad no matter what I did. The hospital plan had failed. Darren couldn't protect me and nor could my family. I couldn't get away from him. I couldn't live with what he was doing. So I grabbed another fistful of tablets and knocked them back with a bottle of vodka I'd sneaked from the cupboard. I thought dying would be my escape from the rapes. They had become a blur, I'd lost count. I wouldn't have to live with this burden anymore. It was all going to finally be over.

In a drunken daze, as Adele played on the stereo, I switched on my laptop. The words of the song, which spoke about how being drunk still couldn't numb her to some-one's touch, seemed aimed at Grandad.

Tapping the keyboard, I started writing, tears obscuring my view of the screen.

Dear Mum and Dad, this is goodbye but please don't feel guilty and don't blame yourselves. I just feel I no longer deserve a place on this Earth. I am sorry for being a massive failure, despite you being the most amazing parents anyone could wish for. I love you. Your loving daughter, Emma.

My heart was broken. I couldn't bear them to know the horrendous truth of the abuse so I didn't mention Grandad. I firmly, stubbornly, was of the mindset that if I told anyone what was happening to me, they wouldn't have believed me and my grandad would come after me even harder. And part of me feared that he'd try to kill himself again. I couldn't handle that, however much I hated him. He was still my flesh and blood.

In my letter, I requested 'Angel' by Sarah McLachlan to be played as my funeral song. I felt the lyrics, about the burden finally lifting, described my life perfectly. It was eerie. I just wanted to find some peace ...

Suddenly, I started retching frantically and my whole body heaved as it tried to throw up the tablets I'd overdosed on. I was terrified. As I felt my life ebbing away, I realised I didn't want to go. Not like this. My parents had gone into town and were shopping for the day. Would anyone find me?

Seconds later, Beth burst into the room. I couldn't stop being sick.

'Oh my God Emma, what have you done?' she gasped, scrabbling for her phone to call an ambulance. She looked as if she'd seen a ghost.

'I'll go to the hospital, but you can't tell anyone about this, promise me,' I cried.

'Ok, ok,' she said, to stop me working myself up into even more of a state. I could count on my best mate to keep this a secret.

I shut my laptop as the paramedics came. I couldn't admit that I'd tried to commit suicide, so I lied to them and said it was accidental. I said I had excruciating stomach pain and it wouldn't go away. I told them I forgot when I last took the tablets. But by the look in their eyes, I knew they had worked out the real reason. At the hospital, they took my bloods and pumped medication into my veins to counteract the effect of the paracetamol. I had to have this for 24 hours.

I repeated that it was an accident; however, the mental health crisis team were called. I told them the same thing but they insisted I took their number.

'Ring us if you ever feel like this again,' they said. Call it pride, shame or denial, but I never did.

Beth didn't know what to say to me. I didn't blame her, though. She assumed I'd done it because I was cut up about Darren and, of course, I let her believe that.

My parents came to see me but I couldn't look them in the eyes knowing what I'd done. They looked haunted.

'Are you taking drugs, Emma? Is that it?' Mum asked, pleadingly.

I shook my head and said I had a bug and had taken a few too many painkillers. She didn't seem satisfied with my explanation but I clammed up after that. They brought me new pyjamas, snacks, drinks, whatever I wanted – morning, noon and night. Inside I was so conflicted. Part of me was upset it hadn't worked, but another part was relieved. I couldn't help but pray they never found the letter, so one day I asked them to bring my laptop.

'So I can watch films on it,' I said. Luckily they didn't know my password so I felt reassured they wouldn't find it and when I got my hands on the laptop again, I deleted my note. The evidence was destroyed.

As the days and weeks ticked by, I felt miserable and an utter loser. I'd failed at trying to take my life, like I'd failed at school, at fleeing Grandad, at everything.

I drank heavily, mostly while out with my sisters, so no one would guess I had a problem. They'd just think I was a wild teenager pushing the boundaries. I hoped I would collapse and die and my bleak existence would end.

At the start of the following year, 2012, my head was a mess. My weight was the lowest it had been – I was now a skeletal size 4. I couldn't stop being sick for the sense of control it gave me. It wasn't about being skinny, it was about releasing the years of pain and hurt I had bottled up inside me.

One freezing January day, I forced myself to go out and ended up joining the throng of shoppers out for the sales. They seemed so ordinary and normal. I longed to swap lives with them. I was so poorly, I needed something to cheer me up so a hit of retail therapy was the distraction I sought.

Heading for New Look, I noticed the security guard stealing glances at me. He was cute with a shy smile. After I paid for some boots and a pair of jeans, he struck up a conversation.

'I'm Chris,' he said, extending his hand.

After chatting some more, we exchanged numbers. He made me laugh – I couldn't remember the last time I'd done that. And he was sensitive, picking up that I was unwell. He made me feel better. After a few weeks of getting to know each other over drinks and meals, he'd always text to check I was ok and kept in touch. A little bloom of contentment grew within me.

We started going to the pub – Chris, Beth and his friend. Again, I kept my budding relationship a secret from Grandad. We had such fun, it became a daily ritual. It helped me to forget everything as I was drinking every day and getting drunk. I would pretend to sleep at Beth's and managed to steal my sister's ID so I could get my hands on booze.

Then my eighteenth birthday came round. Chris came over carrying a sparkly bag. To my delight, he had bought me a backless dress from Miss Selfridge. It was beautiful and I loved it. It was electric blue. 'It brings out your eyes,' he said. I went into town with Beth and had a blast. We got wasted before clambering into a taxi to mine.

Mum was waiting up for me and made us both a cup of tea, asking us how our night was. She let me off being drunk on account of it being my eighteenth, but I could tell she wasn't too pleased. 'Good night, I love you,' I said to Mum when I went upstairs to get ready for bed. The next morning, I awoke with a pounding headache but great memories from the night before.

Two nights later, Chris and I went out alone for drinks. It was a lovely night that I didn't want to end. He made me smile, we danced, kissed and, at the end, got a taxi to his mum's. 'I love you,' he said for the first time and I told him I felt the same. He helped ease my heartache over losing Darren.

I felt happy for the first time in a long time. Chris would take me out for meals or we'd snuggle up together on the sofa with a takeaway on our laps. It wasn't long before we booked our first holiday together – to Ibiza. It was blissful.

Before I went, I'd begged my parents not to tell my grandad about Chris. But to my horror, maybe they forgot, maybe they didn't think I was serious, but they let slip to him, saying: 'Emma's on holiday with Chris, her boyfriend. She's 18 – you have to let her grow up.' When Mum relayed this to me on the phone, I thought my heart would burst out of my chest in panic. They hadn't known what they were doing, but it was about to destroy everything. I knew it was only a matter of time before I heard from Grandad, and when a beep on my phone indicated I'd received a message, I braced myself …

'You fucking lied! How dare you go away with a man. I'm so angry with you, you have broken my heart. I am losing you, I know I am. We will talk about this when you get home.'

In that moment, I knew I was screwed. Finished. The fear I felt inside me made me physically sick.

'Why would he say something like that?' Chris asked, confused.

'It's because he is protective of me,' I said, brushing it off.

When I got back from holiday, I was terrified. I felt trapped – there was no way I could get out of this mess. *Think quickly*, I told myself. *What can I do?*

This is when I decided to hold my wee in for two days. I'd read it would show up as an infection in my blood. I also complained of pain in my abdomen. It was extreme measures, but this was an extreme situation.

I was rushed to hospital, where tests confirmed an infection.

'We believe it is appendicitis,' the doctor said. I felt so relieved. He could not hurt me now. I was safe.

In hospital awaiting surgery, Chris didn't leave my side. My parents and siblings all rallied round, bringing flowers and gifts. I felt so sad that I was making them worry, but I just could not see another way.

A few days later, my op was scheduled. I was nil by mouth and told it was emergency surgery. I felt scared about this. What had I done to myself? Had I gone too far?

When I came round, the doctors told me they were surprised as there was nothing wrong with my appendix; however, they had removed it to be safe. Of course, I knew there was nothing wrong with it but I had to pretend to be shocked. And then I kept making myself sick for a week so I wouldn't be discharged. But in time, I knew I couldn't stay any longer. I had to face the music.

I had not heard a word from my grandad since his text. But when I got home and went for a walk – alone, as Lassie was with my dad – he pulled up beside me. Dragging me into his car, he passed me a sex toy and forced me to use it on myself. I knew this was going to be bad. All the time, he was screaming at me.

'You've hurt me! I can't see you with anyone else,' he shouted. 'I can't bear it, Emma. It will kill me to watch you together. You're mine, you're Grandad's girl.'

He drove like a maniac to the train station, where he picked up a man wearing a suit.

I was made to wear stockings and climb into the back seat. The man got into the back with me. Grandad stopped at some nearby woods and I was marched into the middle of them. I couldn't stop shaking.

Grandad threw down his coat down. 'Lie down,' he barked.

I did as he said as the stranger got on top of me and raped me. It felt like Grandad's punishment for my holiday with another man.

He stood over me and touched himself, revelling in my humiliation and misery. *Look away*, I told myself. I turned to the side, staring into the distance, hot, salty tears rolling down my cheeks. I felt hurt, disgusted and heartbroken. This was all my stupid fault.

Afterwards, we took the man back to his work and my grandad dropped me home. He tried to speak to me like everything was normal and expected me to stop seeing Chris. I felt lost and hopelessly stuck.

Did years and years of this wretched life stretch out in front of me?

Chapter 13

'You don't need to hide anymore'

In a bid to distance myself from Grandad after his last horrific attack, I started staying over at Chris's place. We'd spend time with my family, go into town for drinks and I tried to ignore the gnawing pain and panic swirling inside me.

I took a job at a cafe to help distract myself. It was where I would pop to get coffee before college. I really got on with the plump, warm woman who ran it.

When Chris finished work, he met me every single day without fail and we went shopping for clothes and planned our weekends. For a while, I felt almost normal; like everyone else. But that wasn't to last. One day, my grandad waltzed into the cafe and slammed £100 down on the till. The hair on my arms and neck stood on end, as if electrified. He didn't say a word but the air of menace emanating from him and his cold, black-eyed stare told me everything I needed to know. It was blood money and he was blackmailing me to keep my mouth shut. He was also trying to lure me to his disgusting dogging sites.

As soon as he left, I ran and threw up in the toilets. I felt sick with fear and swallowed a few painkillers to try and numb the terror I'd felt seeing him coming in. I went through the motions until my shift ended and then I headed straight to the pub, downing glass after glass of vodka. I got so drunk, but no matter how intoxicated I was, I couldn't escape the feeling of foreboding and anxiety. It was at fever pitch. I didn't answer my friends', family's or Chris's worried texts and stayed out all night.

At around midnight, I got a taxi to Paula's place. I was a mess. I was hyperventilating and screaming: 'Grandad knows, he knows! Ask him in front of me, go on, ask him.' Paula goggled at me, wide-eyed with fright and confusion. I was wasted and wasn't making any sense. Maybe this was my way of letting some of the truth slip out? Before I could say another word, my grandad, who had been elsewhere in the house, pounced on me, bundled me outside and into the car and drove me home. He was so angry, shouting at me and going crazy that I'd acted out. He was also touching me all over, branding me a slut.

'You can't tell anyone, you need to shut your mouth,' he raged. He had started to notice I was changing. I was becoming a loose cannon and was getting closer to outing his secret. He wasn't going to let that happen.

Pulling up outside my parents' house, Grandad dragged me out and banged on their door. When Mum opened it, she gasped.

'Where have you been? I've been so worried and you've been ignoring my messages,' she cried.

'She's drunk and doesn't know what she's talking about,' Grandad blasted. 'She rocked up at Paula's and woke us up. The girl needs to sort herself out,' he roared.

All I remember after that is racing up the stairs, flopping onto my bed fully clothed and passing out.

The next day, I was feeling like death warmed up, and my parents wanted answers.

'What got into you last night? Why did you turn up at your grandad's at midnight and start getting mouthy?' Dad demanded.

I hung my head. 'I don't know, I can't remember,' I mumbled. Only, I could remember: it was all crystal clear. But I just could not find the strength to tell them.

I started drinking and taking tablets every night to try and block everything out; the abuse, my lies, the immense pain. But no amount of pills or alcohol worked. My life became a miserable cycle of repeated failed overdose attempts, using any tablets I could find – anti-sickness, sleeping pills and painkillers – washed down with spirits. I stopped working at the cafe because the owner and I had a huge fall-out because of the slippery slope I was going down.

I was waking up in hospital more mornings than I could remember. I was slowly killing myself. I would pass out in town and ambulances would be called, and I'd end up in A&E with other drunks and drug addicts. Clubs started banning me because they knew by the end of the night I would be carried away by paramedics. I felt I was losing control. I was in the midst of chaos. Chris couldn't understand why I was so wild and would try and make me see sense. But I didn't care what he said, what my parents said. Mum and Dad were at their wits' end.

'Why in heaven's name are you doing this?' Mum begged. 'What have we done wrong for you to act this way?'

But I remained silent. I couldn't answer. They begged me to stay in and not go out again because they knew what would happen. Yet I wouldn't listen.

One night, while I was staggering about drunk, my grandad grabbed me and shoved me into the car.

'We're going to the Harmston layby,' he barked. 'You have no choice but to do it. I'm not letting you go.'

I tried to shut my body down. A tall, angular man with grey hair around his temples came over to the car, climbed in beside me and started slobbering all over me. I shuddered as he made me touch him under his pants. Just then, Grandad demanded that I touch him too. I felt the urge for tablets and booze. I wanted to die.

A few minutes later, a white van pulled up. Grandad followed the man down into a remote lane, holding my wrist. Suddenly, I was thrown into the back of the van and my clothes were ripped off me. There was a grimy, stained blue carpet, the lights were turned on; there was even a couch and shelves like a tiny living room. I was pushed on the floor and forced to kneel. The man raped me from behind while my grandad attacked me from the front. I felt so worthless, empty and heartbroken and couldn't stop the tears from falling. This was the only younger man my grandad had taken me to. He looked to be in his forties, wore a wedding ring and worked as an electrician. If I'd seen him walking down the street, I would have marked him out as a devoted family man, a new father maybe. He seemed so completely normal. It made what he did to me even worse in a way.

Afterwards, I drank myself into such a stupor I had to be admitted to hospital again. I couldn't pass urine so I had to stay there. I thought: *I'm finally safe again.* Yet despite my extreme lengths, I still couldn't block it out. I made Chris bring me wine and pills up and I took the lot, on top of the IV morphine and antibiotics I was hooked up to. I collapsed in reception and Chris scooped me up, all jutting bones and sallow skin, and tenderly laid me back on my bed. He didn't know why I was hurting myself and I couldn't tell him. I was becoming increasingly unhinged and paranoid.

That night, after one too many questions, I was terrified Chris was spying me. I was scared he was close to finding out the truth about me, about how disgusting I was, so I ended it. He was distraught and I couldn't bear to see him upset, but I couldn't run the risk of him discovering who I was.

My parents were so upset, begging me to stop doing what I was doing and wanting to know why. They wanted to know what was wrong with my mental state. They couldn't understand how my siblings all had the same upbringing and were doing well with their lives, yet I was going down this road and nobody knew why.

And still, my grandad couldn't keep his hands off me. I'd let myself into my friend's flat one day as she had asked me to fetch some of her things before she moved. My grandad knew where I was, turned up and pushed me onto the sofa. It all happened so fast and I couldn't even shout out before he was on top of me and raping me.

Another time, I owed my parents money. Grandad said he would get some cash out to give to me. 'Don't worry, you don't owe me anything for this,' he said, handing it over. Foolishly, I believed him. Turns out that, of course, he took me to the dark, secluded layby and raped me himself. Afterwards, I went into town and got so drunk I could barely walk and kept stumbling over. My sister Lizzie saw me and pleaded with me to come home.

'I don't want to, I'm not drunk enough,' I rambled. I could still feel his clammy touch, smell his nicotine breath on my body and hear his voice shouting at me.

As Lizzie tried to usher me into a taxi, I lashed out and launched myself at her. I don't know why. I thought she wanted me to feel ashamed of my behaviour. Suddenly, the police arrived and pulled us apart. We were both arrested and questioned and when I watched the CCTV in the cold light of the next morning, I was horrified at myself. I was attacking my sister and pulling her hair. I hated myself for it. What had I become? We were released and given an £80 fine, even though it was all my fault. 'Drunk and disorderly' they called it. If only they knew why.

I felt horrible and full of guilt. My sister was furious – she couldn't even look at me and neither could my parents when they collected us both from the police station. We had been given blue tops, joggers and disposable slippers to wear. I looked a mess, like a down and out. I carried my belongings in a plastic bag. I felt mortified. My parents were screaming at me. 'We can't cope anymore. We've tried as hard as we can to talk to you and try and help you but you won't listen,' Dad said, as Mum sobbed beside him.

Dad looked in pain. 'Pack your bags,' he said. 'If you're not going to help yourself and not accept that we're trying to help you, then you will have to learn the hard way.'

'You're kicking me out?' I asked, furious. 'Ok, fine, I don't care. I'll just drink and go out as much as I want then. It's my life,' I yelled petulantly, but I was stung, rejected.

I stayed with a friend and arranged to move to Blackpool and get away from everyone.

My dad rang me saying I couldn't move that far away – it was happening over his dead body. My grandad texted me constantly, pretending to support me but he was preying on me and manipulating the situation. He knew I was vulnerable and had come close to blurting everything out, so he wanted to retain his grip over me. But I was older and less able to be controlled.

A week later, it was Halloween and I went into town, and of course got stupidly drunk. Back at my friend's house, a darkness descended over me. Grabbing a knife, I slashed myself down my arms. It was an attempt to free the pain because I couldn't get the images of the grim dogging sites, the mean old men abusing me, Grandad forcing himself on me, out of my head. I felt completely alone and unable to turn to anyone, so I kept cutting my skin to make myself bleed.

A few days passed, and when I went to the bathroom, I screamed. I was passing blood. Terrified, I called the emergency services, rattled through my symptoms and they told me they had no choice but to send round an ambulance. I rushed around to Paula's. She was at work and Grandad was alone. Despite what he'd done, I felt he was the only one I could call. I'd hurt my parents too much and I didn't want them to see me like this. My belly was extremely painful and bloated.

'I don't know what's happening to me,' I said, explaining the ambulance was coming.

He had a strange look in his eyes. 'You can do this one thing for me first,' he said. 'I'm taking you to the site.'

How could he? I couldn't believe he was being so callous.

I cried out in pain. 'No, I can't! The ambulance is coming.'

He reluctantly conceded he didn't have enough of a window to take me.

At the hospital, I was examined and found to have two litres of urine trapped inside my bladder. They inserted a catheter and hooked me straight on to IV antibiotics. I had a raging infection. My parents rushed over and were shocked at the state of me. My hair was matted, my clothes were ripped and I was stick thin. They brought me new pyjamas, shower gel and my favourite food and drink. When my grandad came to visit with Paula, she started asking me what was going on, as did my parents. I felt ambushed.

'Get out, leave me alone,' I shrieked. They left, but as my grandad turned to go, he looked back over his shoulder, leant into my ear and snarled, 'Your mum and dad hate you.' I buried my head under the sheets.

As the days went by, I started being able to pass urine and felt better in myself, although a dark cloud still hovered over me. I was discharged and started talking to Mum and Dad again. It was awkward at first, but we began rebuilding our fractured relationship.

One Saturday, Mum called. 'I'm making your favourite tomorrow – roast and all the trimmings,' she said. 'I'd love it if you came over. It'll just be me and your dad.'

Something stirred in my heart. 'I'll be there,' I said.

There was a pause. 'Your grandad said you hated us,' she confided.

'That's not true!' I said, incensed. 'He said the same thing about you hating me.'

He'd been trying to fuel the row between us and drive an even deeper wedge. But he wasn't going to succeed, not this time. The ties that bound me to my parents were strong and tightly woven.

'See you tomorrow,' I said, as brightly as I could muster.

'See you love,' Mum said. I thought I heard her voice break for a moment.

I felt happy and excited to see them.

The next morning, I looked awful – pale, skinny and bone-tired. As if I had little life left inside me. But I was determined to make an effort for Mum and Dad.

I brushed my teeth, got dressed in my least crumpled t-shirt and jeans and caught the bus to my parents' home. On the journey, I felt nervous because I had been so horrible to them and they had been worried about me. But I also felt positive because I was going to make things right. At the door, Mum threw her arms around me and Dad squeezed my shoulder. We had dinner and it was lovely, chatting like old times.

After the meal my dad got up and went to bed for a bit. Mum and I continued talking. 'I'm sorry for everything I have done,' I said. 'I want to change my ways.'

She looked shattered, with deep shadows etched under her eyes and her forehead creased with worry lines. There was a chasm that had appeared between us, and I was terrified I wouldn't be able to bridge it. That it was too late and beyond repair. I felt lost; as if I was light years away from who I used to be as a child – the playful, feisty baby of the family with so much promise. That young girl who was so close to her parents, yet who now, at 18, felt further away from them than ever. I hated it. I got the bus back to my friend's. I felt sad to leave but I just needed to go. I felt myself getting choked up and didn't want Mum to see me upset.

Later that night, at around 9pm, everything was still weighing on my mind. Picking up the phone, I rang home. I needed to hear my parents' voices.

'Hello?' said Dad.

'Sorry I didn't say goodbye, I didn't want to wake you,' I said. 'But it looks like I have now anyway. I just wanted to say thanks to you and Mum for dinner,' I continued, feeling strange.

'What's going on, Emma?' he asked.

I couldn't speak, my emotions had constricted my throat. My voice was hoarse and I was rambling. 'What do you mean?' I managed to squeak.

'What tablets has your grandad been giving you?' he said. 'You sound as if you're on something.'

'Nothing, I've just taken a sleeping tablet, that's all,' I drawled.

'Has he given you any heart medication? Because I want to help you but I need to know,' he persisted.

I didn't know why he was asking me this, but clearly he and my mum had been talking and they reckoned my destructive behaviour was down to drugs supplied by Grandad.

'Are you on drugs? Is Grandad giving you pills?' Dad repeated.

He was clutching at straws now. I can only think that he said that because he knew Grandad had access to heart medication and, as I had been acting strangely, he believed it was down to drugs. So they'd guessed he was behind my decline, but not the reason.

Closer, closer …

My heart was pounding.

'No, but there is more to know about Grandad, which I can't say right now,' I continued. It was as if I couldn't stop my words tumbling out. The words I'd kept locked up tight, deep within me, for seven-and-a-half years.

'Emma you can tell me anything,' Dad said, insistent now. 'I will believe you.'

'No you won't, but I will get evidence otherwise nobody will believe me, Dad,' I rambled, the tension ramping up higher.

Closer, closer ...

'Emma just tell me,' Dad pleaded. 'I promise you that no matter what you say, I will believe it. You don't need evidence. You don't need to hide anymore.'

Chapter 14

Truth's out

My heartbeat sped up, building to a deafening crescendo. *Bang, bang, bang.* I half-expected it to burst out of my chest. The drumming filled my ears and seemed to drown out the cacophony of frenzied and fractured thoughts in my head. Dad was hanging on the end of the line, begging me to tell him what was going on.

'What is it Emma? Please talk to me,' he repeated.

But I was stricken with terror. Grandad had subjugated and groomed me so well all these years; his hold over me was still so all-consuming. He'd made me believe it was normal – that this is what all men did to little girls. He'd warned me I'd tear my family's world apart; that no one would believe me and they'd abandon me for good. I'd have no one. Maybe he was right. Who would ever believe such a twisted, preposterous story? Not without concrete proof. But something inside me was fighting back.

'I can't Dad, not yet,' I said. 'I'll have the evidence by 11am tomorrow,' I promised, not really knowing how or what this evidence would be.

But he was persistent now, clearly sensing I was on the brink of opening up.

'Emma, please, what is it? What is it you're trying to tell me?'

I was starting to feel weary, tired of holding in this disgusting secret that was eating away at me and all I held dear, infecting everything I encountered with hate and destruction.

'Promise me you won't tell Mum,' I babbled. I couldn't bear the hurt in her eyes. It was her dad who had inflicted so much pain.

'I won't. Now Emma, what is it? You said, "There is more to know". What has he done?'

In that moment, the floodgates burst open and the truth poured from my lips.

'G-Grandad's been trying to force me to sleep with old men for money ... and him too,' I blurted out, stuttering. 'He makes me work as a prostitute at these dogging sites ... He's made me do it ever since I was 11. Please Dad, don't tell Mum yet. I will have the evidence soon.'

'Don't you dare go near that ... thing again, I don't need evidence. I believe every word,' Dad said, his voice shaking with fury. And then, more softly, 'I believe you, Emma.'

'Thank you Dad, but I have to go,' I babbled.

I had to end the call. I felt as if I was about to pass out because of the surge of emotions flying around my body.

Dad has believed me! I thought, with intense relief. *He doesn't think I'm shameful, dirty*. It was freeing, as if a weight had been lifted.

But then there was blind panic. I thought, *Wait, Dad won't leave it there. He was full of rage. What if he confronts Grandad? What if he hurts him, or worse ...?*

I called up again, crying, and my mum answered. She was sobbing, too. 'I believe every single word of it,' she said through tears. 'It's the only explanation for why you've been how you've been.'

'I am so sorry,' I kept repeating, the emotion threatening to engulf me.

'You've done nothing wrong,' Mum soothed.

I heard a car engine rev in the background and my stomach clenched. 'You're not going to see him, are you?' I pleaded. But Mum calmed me down.

After saying goodbye and telling me they would pick me up in the morning, I felt shattered and numb but couldn't switch off my fevered mind. *I've finally told my parents, and they've believed me!* Popping another sleeping tablet, I fell into a fitful sleep.

The next morning, I felt a jumble of emotions. I was scared of what Grandad would do, relieved that my parents finally knew the truth, but most of all, determined to put my plan into action. It had been taking shape in my head the previous night. I had to trap Grandad once and for all.

My hands trembling, I picked up my phone and started composing a text:

Can you try sort something out with a man? I will do it like before. £50 or even £40 for sex. I just need

the money so bad. We can even do it like we did
before. Delete the text xxxxxxxx

I felt sick and started shaking. Even though I knew I was
setting a trap and wouldn't have to carry out those degrading acts on strangers and feel Grandad's rancid, boozy
breath on my neck, or hear him, panting and moaning as he
groped me, it gave me frightening flashbacks.

Minutes later, a reply pinged onto my phone:

I'll try and I always take the text off as I hope you
do xxxxxx

And then another text:

I enjoy sleeping with you and want it again. I've set
it up for you to go to the site and sleep with men
for money in a couple of days. I've told Paula I'm
at work. I'll pick you up and take you there. I love
you. xxxxxxx

Adrenaline coursed through me. I'd got him.

Ringing my parents, I was on a high, almost manic. 'I
have it, I have the evidence,' I half-shouted.

'We're coming to pick you up,' Mum said.

When I saw Mum, she ran up to me and wrapped me in
her arms. 'You're safe now,' she said.

She couldn't believe what he had done but kept saying that it was the only explanation for why I'd behaved

like I had. Her worst nightmare had become reality. She couldn't understand how he would do that to his own grandchild.

'He's dead to me from this point on,' she said. 'I know he'd been horrible to my mum and cheated on her.'

I had never been told the full story, but had heard Mum say he was a 'womaniser' and that's why her mum and dad had broken up. He had made everyone believe he was this lovely, affable man, but Mum's own dad was a monster for abusing her child. Her father as she knew him didn't exist anymore. Mum felt wracked with guilt – like it was her fault in some way for not seeing the signs, for not protecting me. It was every parent's worst nightmare.

'It's not your fault,' I insisted. 'It was nobody's fault but his. How would anyone ever suspect anything like that? He's your dad, you trusted him.'

All her happy childhood memories were erased. She'd lost her dad. She could no longer recall happy times with him, they'd been consumed by the horror of my revelation.

'You never think this could happen to your family,' she whispered.

We drove to my gran Ellie's and I showed them the messages. I wasn't close to her – Grandad had turned me against her all these years by saying she hated me. She could be stern, but she was also kind. There were gasps and cries. Mum, Dad, Lizzie and Belinda were cuddling me and saying sorry for not knowing and for how much he hurt me. Finally, they understood why I was acting the way I had been. The self-destructive behaviour, overdoses, violence, my disruptive period at school, the moods. It all made sense.

'I don't want sympathy,' I cried. 'How could any of you have guessed what he was doing? And anyway, I kept it well hidden.'

I took a sharp intake of breath.

'I want to call the police now, I'm ready,' I said. Only, when I dialled the number, the words wouldn't come.

'Here, let me do it,' Lizzie said softly, taking the phone from me. Her eyes were puffy and red.

After she'd spoken to the officer and hung up, I looked at Dad. It was the first time I had ever seen my dad, so stoic and tough, cry. He squeezed me so hard and said he was sorry and that he would never, ever let anyone hurt me again.

We went back to my parents' house, and soon two police officers arrived. They had kind eyes.

I sat down and came straight out with it, telling them my grandad had raped me for almost eight years, as well as selling me to men for sex. They looked visibly shocked.

They explained these were very serious allegations and I would have to be interviewed on video at Spring Lodge, a Sexual Assault Referral Centre. That would be in a week's time. In the meantime, they wouldn't be able to arrest Grandad until they had gathered the evidence. We were all in shock and heartbroken. It felt as if we were trapped in limbo, like we didn't know if we were coming or going.

Meanwhile, Grandad was texting me every day and getting increasingly agitated when I didn't respond. Wednesday – the day he'd arranged to take me to the dogging sites – came around and I felt a stab of fear. How was I going to convince him I couldn't go without making him suspicious? Sitting Mum and Dad down, I told them he had lied to Paula about going to work so he would probably still turn up at the site.

I decided I had to show them exactly where he had taken me. A part of me thought they didn't truly believe me yet, and showing them these hateful places where I spent most of my nights would prove to them I was telling the truth. They looked ashen-faced but agreed to drive there. I got in the back of the car and directed them to the site he was most likely to have taken me to, down a remote path near the RAF base. To my horror, he was there. I ducked down and felt sick. My parents looked shaken. They wanted to stop the car and confront him, but I was crying so they agreed to drive off.

Dad was so upset, heartbroken and angry. 'I'll kill him,' he said.

'No Dad,' I begged him. 'I've only just had the strength to come out with this after all these years. What good would you be in prison? I need you now more than ever and I want the world to know what he is and what he has done to me. I want justice.'

My emotions, which had been scattered before, had started to calm down and I could see things more clearly. I knew that I wanted Grandad to pay for what he'd done to me, and if that was going to happen we'd have to keep our heads.

After I'd finished speaking, Dad squeezed me so hard and was crying as if he would never stop. 'Ok love, if that's what you want,' he sniffed.

I decided to stay with my parents and make that my home. We knew we had to wait for the police to do what they had to do.

The tone of Grandad's messages became more insistent and paranoid. It was clear that he was becoming concerned as to why I wasn't answering him and the rest of the family were ignoring him, too. We had to park the car on another street, keep all the blinds closed and go into hiding. My parents weren't sleeping and neither was I.

That week before I was interviewed seemed like a life-time. I felt lost and didn't know what was happening. Everything was going too fast. My head and heart felt bruised and broken. I felt so guilty for tearing my family apart and hurting them as much as I had done. Despite them repeatedly telling me that it wasn't my fault, I didn't really believe them. I'd broken their hearts. I also felt terri-bly guilty for getting Grandad into trouble. He had tried to kill himself before and I feared he might try it again. I didn't want to be the reason a man died in prison. Even though I hated him, I was still heartbroken as I thought his fate was down to me. It weighed heavily on my conscience, making me wake in terror at night, covered in sweat. I couldn't stop crying, hyperventilating and breaking down. At the same time, the scales had finally come off my eyes. I saw everything for how it was as if for the first time – and it felt horrifyingly real.

Mum and Dad were so supportive and told me what had happened was all his fault. 'You did nothing wrong,' Mum said. 'He was the adult, you were the child.'

I still wasn't convinced I was blameless.

My sisters were amazing, too. One day, they sat me down, each of them clasping my hand.

'Why didn't you tell us?' Lizzie asked. 'You could have come to us at any time. We love you Emma, and are so sorry this happened.'

I could see it as I searched their faces. They couldn't fathom how this had happened. They said they were so sorry they were not there for me and that they wished I had said something.

I tried to explain how Grandad had convinced me it was normal, even though every inch of my flesh crept with disgust as he and the others pawed at me. That I thought no one would believe me over him. I felt so ashamed, I told them, and frightened of the repercussions, that I'd locked it away and learnt to detach myself from it. That when I couldn't contain it any longer, I'd lash out or hurt myself.

'We believe you,' Belinda stressed, gazing into my eyes. 'We always wondered why you were the way you were and this is the final piece of the puzzle.'

A couple of days later, it was the afternoon but Mum and I went up to our rooms to sleep. We were physically and emotionally drained. Suddenly, I heard Dad call out.

'He's here,' he hissed in a loud whisper.

He peered through the window and as he'd done so, he'd spotted Grandad's car pull up. I cowered in fright, pressing my ear to the door as I heard them exchange tense words.

'Where's Emma?' Grandad asked. 'I'm worried about her.'

'She's in a mental health unit,' Dad said, desperately trying to think on his feet and protect me. I couldn't have loved him any more than at that moment. 'Yeah, she's lost the plot and we don't know what's wrong. I think it's drugs but they think it dates back to childhood and a top doctor from London is coming to talk to her.'

I could sense Grandad's fear.

'I have to go, I'm all over the place,' he said, before turning on his heel.

Coming up the stairs, Dad said, 'He's gone now, don't worry. He looked scared.'

Chapter 15

'We've got him'

The day of the interview loomed and I was nervous but ready. I arrived at Spring Lodge, not really knowing what to expect. I thought it would be cold and clinical; cheerless. But as I entered, I saw the walls were painted in a sunshine yellow and squashy, pastel-coloured comfy sofas filled the waiting room. I felt instantly more relaxed.

'Would you like a cup of tea?' a friendly receptionist asked.

'Yes please,' I nodded, smiling as I sank into a turquoise couch next to Mum.

A few minutes later, my case worker introduced herself. 'I'm Mary,' she smiled, extending an elegant hand. She wore a baby blue jumper which matched her swimming pool-coloured eyes.

'You can talk to me at any point, or to anyone else here,' she said. 'You can call us about anything at all and we will be there for whatever you need help with,' she said kindly, her voice reassuring and strong at the same time. She explained that they assisted with all parts of the investigation and I would see them every week.

'We are very proud of you for how strong you are in coming forward,' she said. 'It's completely normal to feel it's your fault but it isn't and it never was.'

She was amazing and I suddenly felt a surge of strength rise up within me. The validation of my feelings was so comforting, I found tears of gratitude slipping down my cheeks. I knew instinctively they would be there every step of the way.

A few minutes later, Mary introduced me to Tim, a detective from the Public Protection Unit, or PPU as they called it. He smiled and said, 'Hello Emma, thank you for talking to me. I know it won't be easy.'

Even though I felt stronger, it was still gut-wrenching to know I was about to go through the graphic details of the brutal abuse I'd been subjected to.

Mum wasn't allowed in the room. We hugged and she whispered, 'I love you, darling. Just be honest with the policeman and tell him everything.'

I nodded.

Walking into the colourful room, I noticed the cameras on the walls. Suddenly, I was plunged back to the dirty scrubland and hidden dirt tracks, with a skin-crawlingly ugly stranger's body crushing mine, a look of pure evil glinting in his eyes. Or I was 11 again, pinned down on Grandad's bed, staring at the green and cream striped lampshades as he raped me.

'Take your time, I know this is hard,' Tim said, shuffling some papers in his lap.

I flopped onto one sofa as he sat on another. He was lovely and honest and told me that another detective was sitting in an adjoining room, watching the video roll. He said that after I'd given my evidence, they would arrest Grandad.

'First of all, I need to ask you if you understand what a lie is,' he said.

'Yes,' I nodded.

'If I drew on the wall, said you'd done it and then left the room, would that be the truth or a lie?' he asked.

'A lie, because I hadn't done it,' I replied.

'Ok, that's good,' he smiled.

'Can you tell me how it all started, Emma?' he said softly.

I stared at my hands. My throat felt parched.

'I was 11 when I began staying with my grandad,' I said. 'He'd had a heart attack and my dad brought him round to our house to stay for a little while. After he moved back, I slept over at his during the week, but not weekends as he would drink and later, he stayed with his new girlfriend.

'He would give me fags and alcohol and he began touching me,' I said. I described the grooming and how the abuse escalated to rape over the next few days. I told him that he soon started driving me in his van to meet the men.

As I went through my harrowing ordeal, I caught a rare flicker of shock pass across his face, betraying his usual calm demeanour. But he remained professional and unflappable throughout. Then, Tim asked me questions about the things that had happened to me, for how long, how many men there were and if I knew them.

I couldn't just say 'sex' or 'oral'; I had to go into detail and describe what my grandad and his cronies did to me. I told him they inserted their penis into my mouth and vagina. I was asked to describe the places where he took me and some of the occasions I was made to go to the dogging sites. But there was no way I could describe them all.

'There must have been more than 200 in total, we would be here forever,' I said.

I told him how Grandad made them wear a condom when they had sex with me, about the price list he had for the degrading acts I was made to do. How he'd watch me as they molested me and often joined in. I told him the humiliation and Grandad's threats stopped me from telling anyone.

Once I started talking, it was as if a tap had been turned on. I just couldn't stop. I described how he would take big blue tablets which were called Viagra. I also recalled the bottle of Spanish Fly in his drawer.

'I didn't know what it was or when he used it. I found the little glass bottle in the drawer in the kitchen and when I asked him what it was, he said it was to enhance his friend's sex life. Then after a while it was empty, so I wondered if he'd put some in my drink,' I said. I explained I'd done some research on the Internet and found out the long-term effects of taking it including kidney problems. I mentioned my recurrent water infections and described my suicide attempts and self-harm. It was tough but strangely cathartic, too. I didn't have to hide anymore.

When he asked why I'd come forward now, my voice cracked. 'If I hadn't, I'd have been dead. I would have ended up killing myself and I couldn't do that to my family. I have nieces …' I trailed off, wiping my eyes.

'It's ok,' he comforted.

Tim told me they would first bring him in to question him and then release him on bail while they investigated. They would need my phone to retrieve the messages.

I felt emotional but also detached, because I had learnt how to disassociate myself from the rapes. I understood they had to build a case against him and that's why he would be bailed, but I felt angry and scared, too.

Maybe he would get at me again? I had a recurring nightmare he would take me away and kill me for doing this to him, or that the police would be manipulated by him and believe him and he would be free.

Back home, I was shattered. Every part of my body felt heavy and exhausted. My parents cocooned me in a tight hug and told me how proud they were of me. They were so calm and supportive towards me, but inside I could see it was killing them. Devastated and heartbroken didn't even begin to describe it.

A week later, I was back at Spring Lodge to have internal examinations. However kind the nurses and doctors were, it felt intrusive and shameful. I felt dirty and scared again. They didn't take DNA as I hadn't been involved in sexual activity in the last 24 hours, but I had to have swabs taken from my mouth, vagina, cervix, bum and urethra to check for evidence of rape and also to see if I had any STIs. I told myself I was doing this to get justice; to get Grandad off the streets. I'd gradually stopped myself caring for him since I'd realised the truth, just before Darren and I were about to sleep together, because now I could see him for what he really was. A monster.

After the tests were over, I virtually ran out of the door. I couldn't get out of there fast enough.

A couple of days later, Tim from PPU called me.

'We've got him, Emma,' he said. They'd attempted to arrest Grandad two days previously but he wasn't in. So this time, they'd returned in the early hours to make sure they caught him.

I gasped, hands flying to my mouth. I slumped to the floor, crying with relief and shock. I didn't have the stress of wondering anymore.

Later, when I went to the police station to collect my phone, Tim told me all he'd muttered when they snapped the handcuffs around his wrists was, 'Oh God.' He'd denied everything and accused me of lying. It felt like another punch in the gut. I'd been praying he would admit it and spare me the torture of reliving it all in court, but I was sorely mistaken.

Only, there was a glimmer of hope. 'The text messages we retrieved are really compelling pieces of evidence,' Tim said.

Slowly, my relationship with Mum and Dad repaired itself. In a bid to help distance me from Grandad, my parents asked if they could throw away all my belongings – clothes, toothbrush, knickers, absolutely everything he might have come into contact with – so that I had nothing he had touched or been near. It was their way of trying to do something to help me and I gladly agreed. They bought me brand new things, encouraged me when I said I wanted to dye my blonde hair hazel and cut it into a bob, in the hope it would take some of the bad memories away. Our bond was so much closer and they were hugely supportive. I grew closer to them, opening up about my self-harm. I knew they were fighting their own demons in the wake of the bombshell, but they put everything on hold to help me.

We kept it all within the tight-knit boundaries of our family at first and tried our best to deal with it. I didn't want to broadcast what I'd been through to anyone. My family were all on my side. Everyone had shunned Grandad. Paula was the only one to stand by him, even after she'd heard what had been going on – he'd wrapped her around his little finger. Darren was in the past; Sally I'd lost contact with and Beth, I wasn't ready to tell yet.

The one person outside the family I did confide in was Chris. He was so sorry, like everyone else. He came to my parents to make sure I was ok, but I couldn't look him in the eye so I turned him away. I didn't want his pity or disgust. That's what I believed I could see in his gaze, anyway.

A few days before Christmas, I was doubled up in pain and rushed to hospital. They'd found gallstones and I had to have my gall bladder removed. The hospital brought back so many scary memories for me: Grandad's menacing visits, the times I'd made myself ill and got myself admitted to escape him. I now hated it in there.

My family brought me flowers, sweets and magazines and barely left my side. I was released on Christmas Eve and spent Christmas at home. I was still in pain but it felt comforting to immerse myself in the festivities. We didn't speak of the abuse or mention Grandad for the day. I just needed some normal family time, playing cards, eating chocolate and having fun.

Only just as I thought I was coping, that my patched-up relationship with my parents was giving me strength, things started to unravel again.

It was a month later, January 2013, and the guilt of bringing everything out into the open, coupled with the feelings of shame I was grappling with over the abuse and the aftermath of the bomb that had detonated since I'd spoken out, overwhelmed me. I felt as if I was drowning in an ocean of guilt. I couldn't handle the fact I had told everyone and they all knew my disgusting secret. I felt judged, and paranoid that people were sniggering behind my back. When I went out, I imagined everyone casting disapproving glances and gossiping in hushed tones about me. Above all, I felt terrible for tearing my family apart, hurting my parents and also hurting him – my grandad. I'd convinced myself I'd be the reason behind him dying. I'd be his killer.

So, like a pressure cooker building up steam, I blew. I couldn't handle it. One night, I went out with a girl called Lisa. I'd known her at school but we weren't that close. I was trying to reconnect with people, trying to relive some of my lost youth. I'd started chatting to her on Facebook, had told her about what had happened and we'd become friendly. At some point in the night, I downed sleeping tablets with vodka cherry shots. After that, things turned hazy and I blacked out.

When I opened my lead-like eyelids, I was in a police cell and an officer was sitting opposite me.

'You were in a fight, Emma. Do you remember?' he asked.

'No, nothing,' I said, shaking my head, confused and scared.

I had no recollection of it at all. A total mind blank. I listened aghast as the officer told me there'd been a fight at a club in town called Superbull. Four girls had approached me and I'd hit two of them and they had pressed charges. Lisa had made a statement saying they'd provoked me by harassing us, but it wasn't enough and I was charged. Later in court, I pleaded guilty as I didn't have any memory of it and was convicted of two counts of common assault.

My self-loathing and guilt threatened to engulf me and I took another overdose. The health professionals and my family were concerned for my safety, so the decision was made to section me in a mental health unit. I was so dazed, all I could remember was a doctor, social worker, nurse and my parents surrounding me. Mum and Dad looked bereft; broken.

I had to be admitted to a maximum security ward in case I tried to harm myself. However, after an appointment with the psychiatrist, they allowed me to go for a fag alone. My mind in turmoil, I slipped out my headphones from my pocket and tried to tie them around my neck. I was in a state of anguish and just wanted the pain to go away.

Suddenly, a swarm of people came racing towards me yelling: 'Stop, Emma!' One of them shattered the glass behind which the emergency scissors were kept and struggled to cut off the makeshift noose I'd wrapped around my neck. They'd seen me on CCTV. They saved my life.

After that, I was back in the high security ward. My every move was scrutinised. I wasn't even allowed to wee alone. I had to have someone sat at the bottom of my bed. I hated it, even though I knew it was for my own good and was keeping me alive. I needed help with the guilt gnawing away at me so I was taking the meds they gave me, but they just made me feel numb. My parents were frantic with worry, but tried not to be angry with me. They came to all of my appointments and told me they didn't blame me for anything.

After a couple of weeks I felt more stable and was released. My scattered emotions had settled down but I still couldn't shake the guilt about tearing the family apart and hurting them. I also didn't want to be the reason a man died in prison.

A couple of days before my birthday, Grandad was interviewed again but he replied 'no comment' to every question. It hurt, and it meant he was forcing me to endure the stress of a trial. I was angry he was denying it and making me out to be a liar. It was like his final act of humiliation.

For my nineteenth birthday, we went out for a family meal. I wasn't drinking, and it was nice to finally be together and have a good time. I enjoyed it and felt closer to them than ever. Now the truth was out, we dared to feel optimistic about the future. But I couldn't totally escape him …

One day, while out shopping for new tops and jeans, I whirled around and froze. It was him, Grandad. He didn't say a word but just stared at me. I fought so hard to hold back tears. I turned and walked away as quickly as I could, running into my mum's arms. He should have moved according to his bail conditions, but he didn't. He was tormenting me even now, leaving me shaken up for days.

Meanwhile, my parents made a concerted effort to wrap me in a protective bubble. The same bubble I'd rebelled against when I was a young girl. But now in my fragile state, I needed it more than ever. At least now the secret was out, we would speak about how I was doing and how I felt. It helped ease some of the burden I'd carried for so many years. I was still under strain mentally but my amazing family support network felt like a balm to my frazzled mind.

I was unable to work or study because of my mental health, so I spent most of my time at home. I wasn't allowed counselling because I was told it could throw the case into jeopardy.

'It could bring up repressed memories, things you had forgotten to mention to us, so it could cause issues in the trial,' the detective Tim explained.

Whenever Grandad came up in conversation, Mum and Dad said he was evil and left it at that.

I felt in limbo waiting for the court case to come around. I knew the police had to investigate and build up the evidence against Grandad but the anticipation was excruciating. I had regular appointments at the mental health unit which reassured me and stopped me binge drinking. If I did have alcohol, it would be two glasses at the most. My head felt less foggy and the paranoia lifted.

My relationship with Mum had never been better. She really was my best friend and I could talk to her about anything. When I knew I was spiralling mentally, I could go to her and she would know exactly what to say to soothe me. She came to all of my appointments and was there every step of the way.

Dad, always so strict and stoic, softened after what happened. He became more protective and shielded me from intrusive questions and prying eyes, knowing how much it hurt me to talk about it.

My brother and sisters were also my guardian angels. We became close again after being estranged through the years of abuse. It made me feel incredible and loved. But I never told them about the full extent of what had happened to me. It was too painful and I couldn't bear for them not to see me as their innocent baby sister any longer.

My visits to Spring Lodge were a lifeline. Every week, I discussed the case with Mary and talked about how it was affecting me, my worries about it and how I was doing in general. She was so understanding and cared about my wellbeing. The centre felt like my safe haven. They were the best – so supportive, kind and never judged me. I could call on them at any hour and speak to them about how I was feeling at every step of the process. Unlike counselling, I didn't feel I had to dwell on what had happened; something I wasn't ready for.

Finally, after almost seven agonising months, on 11 September 2013, the police called me. Grandad had been charged with the rape of a child under the age of 13 between February 2005 (the dates are slightly different to those I remembered) and February 2007, sexual activity with a child between February 2007 and February 2012, together with arranging prostitution between February 2007 and August 2012, plus two further charges of inciting child prostitution in January 2009.

I felt an immense wave of relief, elation and freedom wash over me. They knew I was telling the truth – first, the police and now the CPS. Grandad was wrong – I had been believed. The police had also reopened the case of the two girls he'd picked up while I'd been away staying in Ireland. I'd always suspected he had lied to me and he had preyed on them. I felt sorry for them and guilt-stricken, too.

'Maybe if I had come out with it sooner, they wouldn't have had to suffer like I did?' I fretted aloud.

'They're going to bring him down, Emma, don't worry,' Dad said. 'It's going to come to an end very soon.'

Finally, justice was catching up with him …

Sadly, my other attackers would never have their day in court. My grandad wouldn't give up their names – out of spite, most probably – so there was no way to track them down. I didn't know their names, but I'd never forget their faces, however hard I tried.

We celebrated that night with a few glasses of bubbly. Now, it was a case of waiting for the trial. I just wanted it all to be over soon so I could finally get help and start the process of moving on.

Chapter 16

Summer of love

As the weeks and months went by, I opened up more and more to Mum and Dad. We discussed everything he'd done – all the graphic details. I needed them to know, to get it off my chest. I could see the horror, shock and anger in their faces but their love for me grew fiercer and deeper with every revelation.

I had to take the police to the dogging sites so they could photograph them to show in court and so the jury could be driven to the places when it came to trial. I felt an involuntary shiver of revulsion as we stopped by each dirt track or layby, the men's smirking, evil faces popping up unbidden into my mind.

To distract myself from the looming trial, I spent time with my friends. Beth was heartbroken and wondered why I hadn't confided in her. She was upset that she hadn't picked up on anything. Another friend, Tia, had come into my life through college and we would speak every day. She was loyal, supportive and didn't press me too much. It was just what I needed.

College kept my mind occupied. There was always coursework to hand in, classes to attend or an exam to revise for.

I was also spending more time with my sisters, just hanging out together, going shopping and on nights out. They knew me inside out so I didn't have to fill the silence. Sometimes I just wanted to sit without talking endlessly but know that they were near and I wasn't alone.

But I also spent a lot of time by myself, with a book, watching TV, working out in the gym and cooking myself healthy meals. I needed that time to reflect and recover, without outside distractions.

Only, the Friday nights on my own when my sisters and friends were busy began to stretch endlessly. Many of my friends had boyfriends and, one night, I found myself logging onto a dating site.

At first, I wasn't that interested in meeting anyone. I had my family and told myself they were all I needed. And anyway, how could I explain my court case to a potential boyfriend? But after swapping a stream of messages with a man called Nathan, I felt butterflies flutter in my tummy. He was sweet, gorgeous and caring and I found myself excited whenever a new message arrived.

A couple of weeks later, we arranged to meet.

Slicking on my lipstick and slipping on a sparkly black dress felt good. I had already started to like him and felt sick with nerves. What if we didn't click in real life? I needn't have worried, though. We flirted all night, laughing and joking as if we'd known each other for years.

I got drunk for the first time in what seemed like ages, but I felt happy and carefree. He had that effect on me. He was funny, charming and made me feel like the prettiest girl in the world.

'I got lucky meeting someone like you,' I giggled.

'No, I'm the lucky one,' he grinned.

It was the perfect first date, and after that we became inseparable. We'd go out for meals, to the cinema. I quickly fell in love and realised that what I felt for my past boyfriends wasn't the real thing. They were silly childhood crushes. This was real, shout-from-the-rooftops love.

A couple of months passed and I decided to tell him about Grandad. I was so scared of his reaction. I didn't know how I'd be able to cope if the revelations meant he didn't feel the same way about me.

Sipping a glass of wine for Dutch courage, I took a deep breath. 'Babe, there's something I have to tell you, but I'm worried you're going to go off me,' I said.

'You can tell me anything, darling, you know you can,' Nathan said softly.

'It's about my grandad,' I said, biting my lip as if to stop the words spilling out. 'He abused me as a child.' I told him about the upcoming court case looming over me.

Nathan looked horrified and then wiped away a tear. He became upset and squeezed me hard, kissed me and held me close.

'I'm so sorry this happened to you, but this doesn't change anything,' he reassured. My heart swelled with love.

After a cosy Valentine's Day in, I went to Ireland for the weekend with my sister and parents. Nathan and I FaceTimed. I missed him so much. When I came home, he met me while I was out celebrating my twentieth birthday.

While we were dancing, he leant down and whispered in my ear. 'I love you,' he said.

'Don't tell me this if you don't mean it or because you are drunk,' I said. I didn't want to feel vulnerable if he wasn't serious. I didn't know if he was just bandying the words around.

We had a great night and stayed at his parents'. In the morning, he turned over, pulled me close and said, 'By the way, I still love you.' I felt so happy I could burst.

At first, I couldn't say it back because I was scared of tearing down my walls, but eventually I admitted that I did love him. We had an amazing relationship – the affection and passion were uncontrollable. I had never felt a love so strong. He made me forget all the bad things. When I was with him, the world just fell away and it was only him and me. I wasn't the tainted, abused girl anymore. With him, I was perfect.

May of 2014 signalled the start of my Summer of Love.

Nathan and I were caught up in that first, heady rush of hormones and sweet nothings when the world seemed to be painted in technicolour and anything was possible. It had been more than 18 months since Grandad had taken me to the last man and I finally felt safe and free again. Nathan was the perfect distraction from the upcoming trial and just the therapy I needed.

That summer we went on holiday to Tunisia and I didn't want it to end. On the first day we had seaweed wraps and massages at the spa. I felt so pampered. Another day we hired quad bikes to explore the area. Roaring along a rocky path, my brakes failed and I flew over the handlebars. Thankfully, apart from a grazed knee, it was only my ego that was bruised. Nathan managed to keep a straight face until he knew I was ok. And then, out it came; this almighty, garrulous laugh. It was so infectious that soon I was falling about and giggling until my sides ached.

We went parasailing, gliding over the glittery, turquoise sea. I felt like a bird, untethered to my bleak past and soaring towards a brighter future. Nathan was attached to the parachute behind me and I sat in front, drinking in the incredible view. We had a bumpy landing, somehow managing to swerve a group of sunbathers on the beach. It was hairy but hilarious! The next day, we went jet-skiing. We were a little tipsy but so happy. My body tingled as the sea water sprayed my skin and the sun warmed my body. It was the definition of perfect. There was camel and horse riding, which made my legs throb and my bum hurt but I was having so much fun making memories.

We would lie back on our loungers and, because we tipped the pool boy, he brought us pints of beer whenever our glasses were empty. We whizzed down the slide and frolicked like kids in the water. I can't explain how much

I loved this man. I would gaze into his soulful brown eyes and everything would go away.

On the last day, I was reading on my lounger when Nathan came and sat on the end. He looked sheepish and smiled shyly at me.

'What are you up to?' I grinned.

'Emma, I know we've only been together five months, but I haven't felt this way about anyone before ...' he began.

'Oh my God,' I cried, knowing what was coming next.

'Will you marry me?' he asked, sinking to one knee and holding out a gorgeous diamond ring that glinted in the sunlight.

Tears of joy cascaded down my cheeks. I felt like the luckiest girl alive. Yes, it had been a whirlwind, but I was smitten.

'Yes, I will!' I squealed, leaping into his arms.

Back home, I couldn't wait to tell my family, and they were all thrilled for me, knowing how happy he'd made me.

We moved in together shortly after. We couldn't bear to be apart. I decorated with fluffy cushions, rugs and pretty lamps to make the flat our cosy little love nest. He was the love of my life, my best friend, my safe place and the scaffolding holding me together. This was the man I wanted to be with forever. Mum and Dad were so happy for me. They could see the change in me. I'd been a wild party animal but he calmed me down and I preferred quiet nights in over clubbing till dawn.

For Nathan's birthday, I surprised him with a trip to Barcelona. We sunbathed all day and were entwined in each other's arms at night. We couldn't get enough of each other. For our first Christmas in our new home, we both wore novelty elf jumpers and hats. We looked ridiculous but neither of us cared. We were so happy and laughed all day. We went to visit both our families. His parents welcomed me so warmly. Nathan bought me dresses and John Paul Gaultier perfume, while I got him aftershave and clothes. We saw in the New Year together with my parents in town. We were blissfully happy and in love.

A couple of months later in late February, it was my twenty-first birthday. Nathan made me breakfast in bed and gave me a Michael Kors watch. Then, we went out for a family meal and drinks. It helped take my mind off court. The trial had been supposed to begin but it got cancelled again for some reason. My lawyer didn't tell me why.

I wanted to spend every spare minute with Nathan. I wasn't interested in drinking; he was enough. I had so much to thank him for. He was like rocket fuel for my self-esteem and my mental health improved dramatically. He made me feel like a woman, not a pathetic victim.

One night at home, we spoke about the trial.

'Do you think you'll come?' I asked.

He draped his arm round my shoulders and pulled me gently into his arms. 'I don't think I will be able to come, Emma,' he said. 'I'm so sorry but I just can't handle hearing what he did to you.'

'I completely understand, babe,' I said. How could he bear to listen to all those depraved things that had happened to the person he was in love with?

But he was supportive and caring in the build-up to the trial, being there when I wanted to vent or wiping my tears away when it all got too much. I suffered from flashbacks and sleep paralysis, which made me feel as if someone was sitting on my chest and squashing my lungs. It was terrifying. My eating disorder had reared its ugly head again, too. When Nathan caught me throwing up, he was so upset. I hated to see him hurt and knowing I was causing it was the spur I needed to stop it and try and help myself.

Chapter 17

Reckoning

On 23 April 2015 the trial finally dawned – the day of reckoning. I wouldn't be attending until the following morning, because on the opening day the jury were just going to be sworn in. But I was still tense and could barely concentrate, spilling my tea and anxiously pacing the floor of my parents' house. I was scared to death in case he wasn't found guilty. What if he managed to manipulate the jury, just as he'd done with me and my family? As I finished eating lunch – I could only stomach a slice of toast – my mobile rang, making me jump.

It was Tim, the detective. Instantly, I knew he had something major to tell me.

'Hello?' I said, nervously.

'Emma, we need you at court as soon as possible,' he said.

'Why, what's happened?' I asked, heart pounding.

'He's admitted it, everything,' Tim blurted out. I could hear he was smiling now. 'He's pleaded guilty. It's over.'

I burst into tears and ran out into the garden where Mum, Dad and Lizzie were sitting on the patio.

I felt sick – it didn't feel possible. My grandad had admitted that he'd abused me for all those years and sold me for sex. After 19 months from being charged of denying it. I felt as if I would explode with all the pent-up emotion swirling inside me. I knew he hadn't done it for my sake. It was all for selfish reasons. He wasn't stupid and was aware the evidence was weighed heavily against him. If he pleaded guilty, he knew he'd get a lighter sentence.

My family were shocked and didn't believe it at first – they thought they'd heard me wrong. But as it sank in, they rushed towards me and enveloped me in hugs, their tears flowing freely. I called Nathan, who raced round and we both cried.

'You've done it, Emma!' he said.

In a daze, I got changed into my suit. Mum and Dad rang around the family and we sped to court. I was ushered through a secret side door so Grandad couldn't see me. Sat in the public gallery, we all held hands in solidarity as we listened to him plead guilty to all the charges. I felt we were united as a family against him. My emotions spilling over, I started hyperventilating, struggling to catch my breath. Mum squeezed my hand reassuringly.

When the judge looked at Grandad, I could see the anger flame up in his eyes. 'Bail is denied,' he boomed, saying he'd wait for pre-sentence reports before deciding on his punishment. But he said he could expect a long prison sentence.

Finally, I was free. I stood up and my legs felt wobbly and weak. Suddenly, they had gone from underneath me and I stumbled, almost toppling over. My nan and brother grabbed me just in time.

'Take him down,' the judge said. Suddenly, Grandad looked directly at me and smirked. I felt sick and embarrassed that he saw me in that state but I tried to put it out of my mind. It was over. He was a convicted child abuser and I'd won.

Now, we had to await the sentencing in two weeks' time. Back home, we celebrated with champagne at my nan's. I stayed at my sister Belinda's house and the next morning I went home to my fiancé. I needed him more than ever. He was my safe place and made all my fear, anxiety and sadness just fade away.

The day of the sentencing soon came round. Mum didn't leave my side. She was my biggest supporter throughout it all. I could see she was hurt and heartbroken for me, not him. It must have been hard for her seeing her own dad in the dock, but all her compassion was for me.

Seeing Grandad in court, I felt like that wide-eyed little girl who would have done anything for his approval. He still wielded that power over me. *Keep it together*, I repeated to myself like a mantra.

When the judge glided in with his funny grey wig on, the court usher announced, 'All rise.' The whole courtroom got to its feet, before sitting down again as the judge lowered himself into his chair above us, like some stately eagle perching on a branch on high. I could see a huddle of reporters crammed into the press gallery, notepads and pens in their hands, their fingers moving at lightning speed to capture the judge's words.

I knew the case would be splashed across the papers the next day, but my barrister had assured me that, as a victim of a sexual offence, I had lifelong anonymity unless I decided to waive it. Still, it would be weird and unsettling to read about my life in the newspaper and I wasn't looking forward to it.

Suddenly, a hush descended and all I could hear was a muffled cough, the rattle of the ancient heating system and my own heartbeat. I couldn't tear my eyes away from Grandad, stooped but still oozing menace in the dock as he awaited his fate.

Summing up, my barrister Gordon Aspden said that in 25 years at the criminal bar, he could not think of a worse case of child abuse.

He said, 'He abused her to such an extent that she was quite willing to do virtually anything he wanted. She was totally corrupted.'

He said I had been 'a normal, happy child' until I came under the influence of Karl Barker, my grandad.

'She found he was affectionate and always very generous. He would provide her with alcohol, cigarettes and money. It was a gradual process of grooming her for a sexual relationship.'

He'd broken down my barriers by plying me with booze and fags and then forced himself upon me.

He added that after corrupting me, 'he was taking her to dogging sites. She would have sex with strangers for money and there was associated voyeurism.'

He had moved on to even greater depravity, touting me round these places, where other paedophiles would have sex with me after paying him.

'She essentially became a child prostitute, with him acting as her pimp. He often joined in,' said the judge.

They said I was so traumatised, I'd started to harm myself.

It felt odd to hear it spelt out and said aloud like that. But it was validation for all those times I'd been violated and felt devastated, knowing with every fibre of my being that it was wrong, but was told by Grandad it was normal; now I knew with unshakeable certainty that it was depraved and my instincts had been right. It felt incredible to be believed. But I still couldn't help feeling partly to blame. That didn't go away until I had counselling.

Now came the moment of truth.

Passing sentence, Judge Michael Heath told Grandad, 'I struggle to find words which adequately reflect the magnitude of your loathsome depravity. It almost beggars belief that you could do what you did. You groomed her and sordidly abused her and allowed other men, for money, to sordidly abuse her. It is plain to see the effect that has had on that poor girl who is now a young woman.'

He jailed him for 22 years.

Cries of, 'yes', rang out from my family, but I just felt stunned for a few moments.

In a way, it didn't feel long enough, because I had to live with this forever. However, I knew judges were restricted in the length of sentences they could hand down so it was a victory that he would be caged that long.

I thought maybe Grandad would show a flicker of remorse, but instead a sneer played on his lips.

Suddenly, again, my legs buckled and collapsed underneath me. I could barely breathe and I started crying hysterically. That is the last view my grandad had of me. I felt I must have seemed weak and pathetic in his eyes and I couldn't help but feel angry at myself. Mum and Dad reassured me, telling me not to spend a second worrying about what he thought of me. But I couldn't help wishing I'd stared him down and not given him the satisfaction of seeing me emotional. There was nothing I could do about it now, though. It was done.

'He can't hurt you anymore,' Mum said, hugging me. 'He's going to rot behind bars and can't do any more damage. He's no longer a threat to any of us. I never want to see his evil face again.'

She couldn't express how much she hated him.

Back home, I felt a weird mix of elated, relieved and numb.

Everyone I loved was there – Mum, Dad, Nan, my siblings and Nathan. They all looked so happy for me and I pasted on a smile as they told me how proud they were of me, how strong I'd been and how I could now move on and carve out a promising future for myself. How I'd never have to live in fear anymore, how they would always protect me. I was grateful to them for their kindness, I really was.

But I just didn't share their optimism. The future felt uncertain and frightening.

We toasted the sentence with champagne, but it felt like a hollow victory somehow. Yes, he'd been locked up and couldn't hurt me physically, but the psychological scars ran deeper and would need more time to heal.

The next day, I sneaked out of the house to buy a newspaper. My mum and dad had tried to shield me from press coverage, but I was curious and needed to know. Among the reporting of the court case, my eyes fell on another article: *'Child rapists who abused girl, in Lincoln, will never be caught'*, screamed the headline.

My heart sank. I'd feared the other men who had molested me would escape justice but to see it in black and white like that was a blow. I never saw the other men from around town, which got me thinking that perhaps they might have travelled from neighbouring towns, making them harder to identify.

I read on. It said that the head of child protection at Lincolnshire Police had stated that the only way to snare the other men now would be if they were to hand themselves in.

He said, 'The poor girl didn't know these people at all. It was horrific – not only the abuse that was suffered but the brazenness of it all. The fact that other people participated in it too is unbelievable. They must have known that the girl was young. It beggars belief.'

The superintendent added: 'We would like to say we were still investigating this but we're not, because when the initial offences were reported they were already historic and the abuse went on over quite a long period. We have no forensic opportunities, which makes it difficult for us.

'To treat a victim in this way, and for the males to participate in it, is unbelievable. It's an understatement to say the impact on the victim has been life-changing. The fact he had sex with her was bad enough – but to then take her to those sites is not something we see very often.'

I didn't blame the police. They'd been fantastic and their support meant the world. I laid the blame squarely at Grandad's door. Withholding those names had been his final, petulant, act of control over me. Even from the dank depths of his prison cell, he had known just how to get at me.

Chapter 18

Blue Lines

Once the court case was over, Nathan and my family co-cooned me into their protective fold. I needed cosseting for a while because I felt as if I had been thrust into a new and uncertain future and was blinded and overwhelmed by the myriad possibilities that lay ahead. I'd been reborn but with that came challenges and questions. For such a vast chunk of my childhood and teenage years, I'd been Grandad's sex slave. Could I emerge from that world unscathed? Would it always be a part of me and how would that manifest itself? What was my purpose now?

I tried to still my mind and not peer too far into the future because it frightened me. Instead, I focused on my relationship with Nathan, which had anchored me and provided safe harbour, and applying for a new college coun-selling course, something I wanted to do just for myself.

I couldn't bear the thought of other survivors of abuse, or those who had undergone any sort of trauma, to be feeling like I had. I wanted to help anyone who was struggling because I knew first-hand how much it hurts to feel broken and lost. I put aside my childhood dream of being a children's nurse; helping survivors of abuse and trauma felt more important now. It was like a calling. I was on the waiting list for counselling for myself – I wanted to try it but I was apprehensive about it, too. I didn't want it to bring up feelings and memories I wasn't ready to face.

For the first time, I had the confidence to start driving lessons, and when I passed I leapt with joy. It gave me a valuable sense of independence and freedom. I felt so free behind the wheel and proud of myself.

Nathan surprised me with tickets for a holiday on a Greek island with his family. We made our way to the airport in two cars – Nathan and I in one and his Mum, Dad and sister in the other. I had never been so happy or excited about something.

After checking in, we sat in the VIP lounge sipping wine and eating croissants. Nathan's family were lovely and chatty and included me in their conversation. On the plane, Nathan and I got giggly on champagne. I felt so carefree and frivolous.

Our hotel room was huge and bright with a sea view. We soon slipped into a blissful routine; a breakfast of Greek yogurt topped with honey in the morning, followed by drinking and playing ball in the pool. Later, when the scorching midday sun passed, we strolled to the beach, where we'd hold hands and listen to music. We stacked lilos on top of loungers to make them comfier. I flicked through a trashy beach novel and, at night, we all went for meals together, the whole family.

Nathan and I had one day to ourselves. We hired a buggy and drove around all day. In the evening, we went for a romantic dinner against a flaming coral and pink sunset. Entwined in each other's arms, we spoke about trying for a baby. It thrilled me to think we could create a new life made up of both of us.

Maybe this is my reward for surviving, I thought.

Two weeks zipped by much too quickly and I didn't want to return to reality. But once I'd landed back in the UK, I realised I was excited to come back to my counselling course.

On the first day, my tummy swirled with butterflies from the moment I woke up. I was so nervous yet so excited to start. I was finally living my life for me and I couldn't wait to take it by the horns. I pulled on my leather, snake-skin print trousers and a long white shirt. I added a slick of pink lipstick.

When I arrived, the other new students looked just as scared as I did. We had to sign confidentiality agreements so whatever we spoke about during the lesson was kept within those four walls. This made me feel at ease. I'd been worried about sharing my experience but knew I had to be a little vulnerable, for my own healing and to be able to help others.

When it came to telling the class about what had happened to me, I kept it brief, but my heart was drumming wildly in my chest. I was worried they would shun me because they wouldn't know what to say, but they were all supportive. They listened and thanked me for sharing and we moved on, with another student opening up about their experience. If they were shocked, they didn't show it. It was not a massive conversation and I was glad.

The course rapidly became my lifeline. It gave me some stability and I felt a sense of purpose burn strongly inside me, knowing I was pursuing a rewarding path. It also got me thinking. This was the first time that I'd studied without being bullied or getting into trouble. It felt empowering and made me proud. I *could* stick to something and apply myself. I was capable. It gave me the biggest boost.

The course covered an introduction to the different types of counselling and we were given insights into theorists such as Sigmund Freud. A key part of the course was to keep a journal, which allowed me to analyse my feelings about how studying counselling theory made me think about my own life experiences and how they had affected me. I had to dive deep into my emotions and it wasn't always easy, but the self-awareness and sense of personal power it gave me was invaluable. I learnt so much about myself and my qualities – such as my empathy, strength and listening skills.

Nathan was by my side when the police called and said Grandad had lost his appeal against his sentence, in November 2015. I knew he would try as he had nothing to lose. But reading the news reports made me bristle with anger and I felt a fresh hatred rise up inside me.

A Lincoln pensioner who repeatedly raped a vulnerable 12-year-old girl before turning her into a child prostitute has been told by judges he richly deserved his 22-year sentence.

Judges at London's Criminal Appeal Court 'struggled for words to describe the loathsome depravity' of Karl Sinclair Barker, 69.

Lord Justice McCombe threw out his complaints, saying he had shown no remorse and had committed crimes of almost 'unbelievable awfulness.'

My stomach clenched as I read.

'He displayed no victim awareness and doesn't believe he forced his main victim into anything,' said the judge.

'He failed to appreciate how wrong his actions were ... The sentence of 22 years was appropriate for the severe harm caused. These were offences of loathsome depravity.'

I quickly shut the newspaper and shivered. *Good riddance*, I thought.

Later that day, my family all gathered at my gran Ellie's. I'd never been that close to her but since the case, she had told me how sorry she was and reached out to say I could call her if I ever needed her. We were all just happy and relieved it was over and that we could start to rebuild our shattered lives again. But just when I thought things were turning a corner, the rug was whipped out from under my feet …

After a blissful start, cracks appeared in my relationship with Nathan.

At first, they were hairline fissures, but over time, they grew deeper. We were arguing a lot and Nathan seemed to prefer nights out with his friends over spending time with me. He'd been my rock throughout the run-up to the case, maybe it had taken it out of him and now he was wobbling? Whatever the reason, there was no denying we were going through a rocky patch, so we decided to have a break and he moved out. I was heartbroken and missed him desperately, but I threw myself into my studies and surrounded myself with family.

I'd never lived on my own, but I felt so independent learning how to budget the household bills and I took pride in making it feel like home by decorating it with family photos, cushions and colourful prints. I even bought a dog, Rocky, who became my constant companion.

Then, just as I started to feel stronger, I had a shock. I was pregnant. Two bright blue lines on the test I was clutching confirmed it. When we had been together, Nathan and I had been trying, but it had proved difficult because of my polycystic ovaries. And now we'd split up, it had happened. It didn't seem fair.

I told Mum and Dad straight away. They were upset and worried as to how I'd cope, but vowed to support me. Next, I psyched myself up to call Nathan. How would he take it? After a long, stunned pause, he said he was shocked but happy, that he'd always loved me but just got selfish and been immature because he wanted to live the single life. But the thought of being a dad had shown him what he really wanted. He said he'd support me whatever I decided.

'We can't get back together just for the sake of a baby,' I said. So we agreed to go slowly. I felt excited that maybe this was part of the purpose I'd been searching for. But I was also so scared. Nathan and I weren't totally secure and I had my course to do. But I would have to manage somehow. I could never get an abortion. It went against my faith and didn't sit right with me.

One day, I was going to bingo with my mum and I turned into a junction. I misjudged the gap and a car crashed straight into the side of me and my car spun 360 degrees. I smashed my head on the window and Mum suffered whiplash. I was frantic, screaming, 'My baby, my baby.' Luckily, it was unhurt.

Around this time, I'd started being plagued by flashbacks of the last time I'd seen Grandad in court. I couldn't help feel that he'd thought I was weak because I'd showed emotion. If only I could face him in prison and prove to him that he hadn't broken me. So the next time the police liaison officer popped round, I broached the subject.

'I want to see my grandad,' I said. 'I want to regain my power and control. He always belittled me and owned me and he relished it that he almost broke me. I want to go in and show how far I have come mentally and in my life.

I want to know why he targeted me. But above all, I want him to know he didn't break me, he did not win and he never will.'

After I'd finished speaking, I realised I had tears in my eyes. The officer looked moved.

'There is a restorative justice scheme which I can put you forward for,' she explained. 'It gives victims the chance to meet with their offenders to explain the real impact of the crime – it empowers victims by giving them a voice. It also holds offenders to account for what they have done. But there are no guarantees he'll agree or even if the prison authorities will give it the go-ahead.'

I knew it would be one of the hardest things I'd do and that my parents would be upset, but I didn't hesitate.

'Please put me forward. I want to do it,' I said.

On my twenty-second birthday, Nathan's parents had gone away so I went round for a takeaway and film. I stayed the night. It was like when we first met. I felt content as I stroked my blossoming bump. When I woke up, he handed me a card with pictures of us and the scan photo. To someone else, it might have seemed cheesy and stupid, but to me it was perfect. Later, I went for a meal with my family. Everyone was drinking but I didn't mind not being able to. I was growing a baby inside me. Not just any baby, but mine and Nathan's. I felt a thrill of plea-sure knowing this.

On Mother's Day, my mum got me a beautiful card from my unborn baby and wrote a poem inside. Tears trick-led down my face as I read the sweet words:

Mummy can you feel me, I'm wriggling for you

I can hear you say you love me, Mum I love you.

Very soon you'll meet me, and kiss my little face

And I will feel your warm skin, and admire you
for your grace.

Mummy are you ready, my life is just about to
start

I will hold your little finger, but you will hold
my heart.

Then, at 17 weeks pregnant, something happened that shattered my world. I started to bleed, and Mum rushed me to hospital where I was told I'd lost my baby. I heard a blood-curdling howl and realised it was coming from me.

I had to give birth. My body just went numb. It was a beautiful little boy. He looked as if he was sleeping. I named him Lucas and loved him with every inch of my being. I had to say goodbye but I couldn't let him go.

You'll always be my first, I mouthed, kissing my index finger and placing it on his forehead. *I will never forget you.*

Mum was with me, trying to comfort me. I'd rung Nathan but he hadn't picked up. I felt heartbroken I'd had to give birth to my sleeping baby alone. Why had I been put through so much? What had I done wrong to deserve all this?

For a long time I slept clutching a little box to my chest. It held all that remained of my lost child: my baby's hand and footprints that the hospital had given me, alongside a tiny blue woollen doll's hat. Sleep was fevered and full of nightmares. Often, Grandad's face would loom into my mind, his eyes demon-like and blood red and I'd wake screaming and bathed in sweat. Grieving over my loss, and angry with my grandad for haunting me even in my dreams, I couldn't take much more. Mum had been keeping an eagle eye over me but my emotions were just too overpowering and threatening to engulf me.

Seeing the pain etched in my face, Mum squeezed me tightly and cried silent tears. 'I'm so sorry, my love,' she said. 'If I could take all this away, I'd do it.' She was distraught, too. She'd lost a grandson.

A couple of months passed and acceptance slowly sank in. I realised that I'd lost my baby due to intolerable stress and that he was really gone. I'd never hold him, see him smile, help him with his homework or blow him kisses. But I realised I could get through this. With Nathan and my family's help, but also through my own strength. I'd surprised myself by finding I was much more resilient than I'd given myself credit for. The skills I'd learnt on my counselling course also helped me, such as strategies for self-compassion, not letting emotions overpower me and challenging negative feelings by writing. Keeping a journal, where I could free my innermost thoughts, was really helpful.

I started therapy in 2017 – two years after Grandad's conviction, because there had been fears I wasn't ready before then. After learning about counselling, I was eager to try it and hoped it would help me work through the trauma of the abuse. But it brought back repressed memories; horrors I'd locked away deep in the recesses of my mind. I started to experience terrifying episodes of sleep paralysis, where, as well as the scary voices and shadows that plagued me, I saw my grandad grabbing me and mocking me. This would happen as I fell asleep, and I became so terrified I'd stop myself from closing my eyes. I realised I hadn't found the right form of counselling for me, and I decided to wait and revisit it in the future.

For my birthday that year, in 2017, Nathan and I went to York. On the first night, we had a meal in the pub with lots of red wine and watched a boxing match. The next morning, disentangling ourselves from each other's arms, we prised ourselves out of bed, went for breakfast and visited the dungeons. Nathan moved back in soon afterwards.

We had a heart-to-heart and he apologised for his past behaviour. He said he was silly and immature and didn't realise what he was doing to me until I was no longer there.

'I'm so sorry for all the pain I have caused you. I've been an idiot and wasn't worthy of you. I will now spend every minute I am with you showing you that I love you and have learnt from my mistakes,' he said.

So far, for almost two years, he has stayed true to his word.

Chapter 19

A good place

For now, the love and understanding of Nathan and my parents, as well as the care of staff at Spring Lodge, is what I need. At Spring Lodge you don't feel like you're under pressure and you are not asked to bring up topics you don't feel comfortable with. Everyone there knows me and always has time for a chat. You're not just another person. I have one support worker, so there is consistency, but I have got to know several of the people and they are all really supportive. I always feel that I'm welcome there and there's always someone I can talk to, even now after the case is over.

The police and my barrister have also been amazing and have said I can call them anytime, day or night. They became invested in my case and said they were so proud of me that I'd found the strength to speak out and bring him to justice.

My barrister pushed for me to receive compensation from the Criminal Injuries Compensation Authority, something I didn't even think I was entitled to and didn't want it; I felt it would be tainted somehow. But my parents said I deserved to have my future laid out, the career I dreamt of and the money for any future therapy. I was turned down because of my criminal record, something my lawyer is fighting to overturn. As he stated in my defence, the only reason I have a conviction is because it was committed when I was in Grandad's grasp and was solely down to the impact of the abuse on my behaviour.

Last summer, the spectre of Grandad came to haunt me again.

I was at a family barbecue. It was a lovely, special day, with the sound of tinkling laughter and the satisfying sizzle of meat cooking on the grill. As the evening slipped by, confession was in the air. Suddenly, I heard a loud sob and turned to catch sight of a family friend I didn't know very well, Fiona, running away.

'What happened, Mum?' I asked later.

'Fiona said, she said …' Mum trailed off, before recovering her composure. 'He abused her too,' she blurted out finally.

My heart shattered for her. He made her feel so dirty and ashamed, she buried it for decades. Mum told me Fiona thought he'd raped her up to three times when she was around ten. She didn't feel ready to tell the police.

So I wasn't Grandad's only victim. I'd always known I couldn't have been the only one, that someone with sick urges like Grandad's would have struck before. But it was still devastating to think he'd destroyed another person's childhood.

Another blow sent me reeling. I was called to a meeting at Spring Lodge, where the restorative justice worker who had been trying to get me a meeting in the prison with Grandad sat me down. 'We have tried everything we can, but the prison doesn't think it's a good idea,' she said.

I held my head in my hands. It felt like Grandad had won. It was heart-breaking because they hadn't even asked him if he would agree to meeting me. If he had said no, I would know he wasn't man enough to face me. But the prison authorities made the call, deciding that they knew what's best for me. I'm not giving up that easily, though. I have the restorative justice worker and Spring Lodge in my corner fighting to change this and I have contacted my MP. My parents are also supportive, even though they didn't want me to see him at first, understandably after the destruction he'd wrought on our lives. They couldn't disguise that they hated it but once they realised it was something I needed to do for me, they tried as hard as they could to support my decision.

I recently got some good news. My complaint has been escalated to the police and crime commissioner and there are set to be talks to discuss changing the service so victims, and not the prison service, have more of a say about facing the perpetrator in prison, as long as they feel ready and have been assessed. It felt as if he had more rights than I had. I couldn't call him a monster in my letter of application for the restorative justice scheme in case it affected him mentally. I couldn't believe how topsy-turvy it was. So hopefully, my case can be the catalyst for change and help shape new policy.

As for Grandad, he will never be sorry for what he did. For stealing my childhood and my innocence and leaving me with deep mental and physical scars. He's only sorry he's been caught. It pains me to say it, but I don't think he'll die in prison. Now he is in there and forced to take his heart tablets and not drink to excess, he might make it out. It's not something I want to contemplate for long.

Why do I think he targeted me? I have gone over this time and again. Was it because I was vulnerable and easy pickings for a paedophile? Because he could see I was the youngest and felt drowned out by my elder siblings? That I longed to feel grown-up and as if I mattered, so he latched onto that, grooming his Grandad's girl for his wicked abuse? Or was he a psychopath, pure and simple, and I was unlucky enough to be in his sights? The truth is, I could speculate endlessly and drive myself mad. If I knew the reason, I wouldn't need restorative justice.

I feel catastrophically let down. If my doctor had asked questions when I was just 11 years old and examined me, Grandad could have been stopped. They should have more awareness of the signs of sexual abuse. If my school had done more to protect me and investigated more thoroughly why my behaviour had become so aggressive and violent, if they'd told my parents when Grandad changed my home address to his, or on the countless times he took me out of school to bundle me to the dogging sites and flagged this to social services, he could have been stopped.

But they failed me.

I came from a good, loving home. Did the authorities feel something like this couldn't happen in a family like mine? But that shouldn't matter. This can happen to a child in any family – poor, privileged and everything in between.

In my future, I see marriage and children. I don't know for certain if it will happen but it's something that I feel will give me a purpose and what I was put on earth to do. I will be a protective mum, as any parent should be, but I will resist keeping my children in a bubble and allow them to breathe. Of course, I will have a heightened awareness of the dangers children face. One day, I will have to break my own heart when I sit down with my children and explain what happened to me.

I'd also like to talk to Fiona, although I understand she's not up to it right now. Sharing what happened with someone who can empathise because they experienced it too will be incredibly powerful in both our journeys towards healing.

After doing my course, going back to a new therapist and reflecting, I have finally stopped blaming myself. I tell myself it was only Grandad and his cronies that have to bear responsibility. But still, I have good days and bad. I will have a couple where I feel alright and strong, and then, on the low day, I'm hit with flashbacks of the times my dignity was stripped from me and I was left bloodied, broken and discarded in the backs of vans. It makes me sick; I will cry and get angry. Then, I'll blame myself and wonder why Grandad did this. I can't help but ask myself whether I led him on even though I know I didn't because I was a child and he was the adult. However, on these bad days, I seem to forget this and blame myself for everything, even hurting my family.

I'm often asked if I feel frustrated with my parents for not noticing, but my answer is always an emphatic 'no'. Their background and upbringing, plus the fact I hid it so well and Grandad was a skilled manipulator, I believe made it virtually impossible for them. But if I could offer advice to parents, I would ask them to look out for the signs of abuse. Explain to their children to never keep secrets from Mummy and Daddy and that what's in their pants or knickers is theirs and nobody should ever see that.

After three years of study, including placements in which I have helped people going through trauma, something which I've found hugely fulfilling, I am now a qualified counsellor and I plan to go on to university to do my psychology degree and eventually became a psychologist. I'm giving myself the education I should have had at school but that he robbed from me. I can't begin to imagine how rewarding it will feel to help others who have suffered traumatic experiences and guide them out of the darkness and towards hope. I have helped the police and Spring Lodge in their campaigns to raise awareness of child sex abuse – something I will continue to do for as long as I live.

I work on my mental health every day and I am rebuilding myself and my future without Karl Barker. I want to better myself, to love and respect myself. I want to find happiness and never allow anyone to hurt or abuse me again. I take time each day to tell myself not to be so hard on myself. I have been through enormous turmoil by the age of 24 and it's ok to not be strong all the time.

I will also do my utmost to fight for children against monsters. To survivors of abuse, I want to say that it is ok to be scared, it is ok to blame yourself, but you need to know that there are people out there who once blamed themselves too, but they found the strength and told someone what they'd been through. The support you will receive is unexpected yet so powerful.

It's really difficult to come to terms with what's happening and really hard to come forward and tell people. You have all these worries and doubts about what people will think and what they'll say. What if no one believes you? But you're never going to know until you come out and tell someone, and those fears are never going to stop. Your life's never going to get better until you take that step. I'd tell other people to try and get help and support from the right people as early as you can.

The secret ate me alive so much that I had no choice other than to come forward. I had developed an eating disorder, self-harmed, overdosed numerous times and tried to take my own life on several occasions because I felt so guilty. I was sectioned and I was violent because I didn't think I needed to be in there, but actually, at the time, I did.

Telling my parents was the hardest thing but they both believed everything I said. My parents knew something was wrong but they just didn't know what. I think it was like a missing piece of the jigsaw for them – they couldn't understand why my behaviour had been so bad.

Before I reported the abuse, I didn't think anyone would believe me, but the support I've had has been unreal. I thought I would lose people in my life but I actually gained people who truly care. Because everything is out in the open and it's like a whole weight has been lifted, I feel as if I don't have to hide anymore.

When you've been sexually abused, especially by someone you know, they make you feel ashamed and guilty, like it's your fault, but it's not. It's about control and manipulation. They'll turn things around on you and say 'you made me do it'. They try and get into your head. Grandad told me that my mum and dad hated me but that he would look after me. He gave me money and said he was the only person I had.

I had been dreading court, but my Spring Lodge support worker came with me. While you're waiting for the case to be heard, you are protected and safe. There are different options – I was taken through a separate passageway so I didn't have to see Grandad before court. You can do a video link if you want to. Support workers can come into the witness box with you now, too.

I'm actually in a really good place now. I know I'm not the person he knocked me down to be. I'm so much stronger. I think I chased love after what happened to me and my relationships suffered. Even though Nathan and I are happy, I know that whatever happens in the future, the love of my family will endure. I have surrounded myself with good people.

I can openly cry now, something I never allowed myself to do, and it is truly healing. Trying to live with something like that on your own is like fighting a losing battle. It's horrible. If I hadn't told someone I don't think I'd be alive today.

I went through one of the most deplorable and disturbing things a child could experience, but by writing this book I want to show that ultimately my story is an inspiring one, because of how much I have achieved and how much I still want to do.

Remember that you deserve to be happy. You deserve to be free from guilt. You deserve to know this is not your fault and you deserve to be free.

Epilogue

I'm still waiting to hear if I will be granted a meeting with Grandad behind bars. It's not something I'm consumed by as much as I used to be. That's down to how much more confident I feel because of everything I have achieved since the verdict. The strength I've drawn from the support of my family and close friends, my counselling qualification and the cathartic process of writing this book, mean I don't obsess over it like I once did.

I do, however, think about what I want to say to him and to show him I am no longer broken. So I decided to get some of those words down on paper. This is my letter to my grandfather. Until I get the chance to look him in the eyes and tell him how far I have come, this is the next best thing.

To Grandad

When I was little, I absolutely idolised you. You never forgot my birthday, you helped me when I got five pence stuck inside my nose, you made me feel special. I was Grandad's girl and you were my hero. You were my grandad and you should have protected me. But you failed to do this one thing. But I want you to know that you did not destroy me completely, however hard you tried. It has taken me a very long time to finally accept what you did to me and who you really are. I could never admit it until I got you arrested. You see, I still thought I loved you then and blamed myself.

You told me it was normal, that you were my grandad and you would never hurt me, that I should trust you. I believed you. I know now that it was all a web of twisted lies and actually, I wasn't stupid or gullible for believing you. You escaped justice for a long time, but your day of judgement arrived when I stood up and told the world what you had done to me.

I remember that day you first laid your hands on me when I was just 11 years old as clearly as if it had happened yesterday. But I'm winning now. Those memories don't swarm into my mind like they used to. I used to live in fear. I used to live in shame. Now I live in strength, happiness, acceptance and I face the world with a kind heart. After what you did, my achievements become nothing short of miraculous.

I used to ask myself, Was it down to me? Was it my fault somehow? Did I lead you on? For a long time, I could never have answered these questions but now I can. I realise that this was never my fault. How could it be when I was a young, innocent child, not even into my teens? How could I lead you, a grown man, on? I wasn't dirty. You were the adult in this situation and you had manipulated me to such an extent that I thought this was normal. There is no conceivable excuse for what you have done to me and how you made me feel, for how you broke my parents' and siblings' hearts.

When I finally opened up, I was petrified because you made me believe nobody would listen to me or take me seriously. But when I found the strength and courage to tell my parents they believed me straight away. My mum said it was the only explanation for why I had been how I had.

I trapped you into admitting it all on text messages. I guess I wasn't that silly little girl you used to tell me I was because it's those texts that helped the police catch you. I turned the tables on you and helped secure a successful police prosecution. You told everyone I was lying. You kept up your act, trying to fool the world into believing you were the innocent party. The ones that loved and knew me never even questioned me. They knew you had done this. Two years and four months after your arrest, you finally admitted it. You put the family through even more anguish by pleading guilty only on the day of the trial.

You have only ever seen me weak, vulnerable and scared of life. I'm writing this today to tell you that you could not be more wrong about me. I'm so different now. I'm so much stronger, I can stand tall and proud and tell my story because it's not a story of weakness or abuse. This is my story of survival. I will fight for children and stand with campaigners against abusers like you to make sure they will never win.

I'm a counsellor now so my experience in the world you forced me into will help other children come through their ordeals. Nothing will ever break me – especially not you. You hardly even cross my mind these days and when you do, it's when I tell people to remind them that no matter how bad life gets, you can always fight to survive.

I won. I broke free and now I'm flying high. I have my freedom. I have my success. And most importantly, I have my strength.

I used to hate you. However, I've grown so much that I no longer do. Do you know why? If I hated you, that would mean I was still holding onto the memories; to you. I don't feel anything whatsoever towards you. The only person I do feel something for is me. I feel so proud of myself for still being here, forging a bright future for myself.

I hold my head up high and I no longer feel ashamed. I'm turning around and walking away from my past, into a happier and hopeful future.

Emma

Acknowledgements

I would like to thank my wonderful family, especially my parents and siblings, who have been amazing. I don't think I'd have been able to come as far as I have without their help.

The support from Spring Lodge has been a lifeline. I would also like to acknowledge Tim (false name) from PPU and his colleagues, who have shown me huge respect and support throughout the whole process.